HEART
OF A
MOTHER

BOOKS BY WAYNE HOLMES

The Heart of a Father
The Heart of a Mother

WAYNE HOLMES has served as a children's and youth pastor. His writing has appeared in periodicals and *Ripples of Joy*, a story collection. He is the director of the Greater Cincinnati Christian Writers' Fellowship. Wayne, his wife, Linda, and their family live in Cincinnati, Ohio.

The HEART
OF A
MOTHER

true stories of inspiration
and encouragement

Compiled By
WAYNE HOLMES

BETHANY HOUSE PUBLISHERS

Minneapolis, Minnesota

Published by Bethany House Publishers
11400 Hampshire Avenue South
Bloomington, Minnesota 55438
www.bethanyhouse.com

Bethany House Publishers is a Division of
Baker Book House Company, Grand Rapids, Michigan.

Printed in the United States of America

Library of Congress Cataloging-in-Publication Data

The heart of a mother : true stories of inspiration and encouragement / compiled by Wayne Holmes.
      p.   cm.
   ISBN 0-7642-2805-6 (pbk.)
   1. Mothers—Religious life.   I. Holmes, Wayne.
BV4529.18.H43   2003
242'.6431—dc21   2002155878

DEDICATION

TO
my mother,
Joyce Elaine Holmes

ACKNOWLEDGMENTS

The concept for this book is a simple one: By taking a look at the lives of earthly mothers we can get a glimpse into the heart of God. A simple undertaking—or so it would seem.

While in the process of putting together this collection of stories, it dawned on me that I didn't have a story of my own to tell. I tried to reach back into my childhood and pull up a memory of a time in my life when my mother did something that inspired me and led me to understand the personality of God. No such memory came to mind.

I chatted with my brother Walter about the lack of a personal example.

"I couldn't come up with anything either," he said. "She's always been there—doing the things that mothers do." I nodded in agreement. "Perhaps that's just it," he continued. "She's always been there, consistently providing for our needs, supporting us through good times and bad times, believing in us, and loving us no matter how much joy or grief we've given her. Isn't that just like God?"

The question needed no answer. Of course she has, and continues to be, a living example of unconditional love in action. She—and all godly mothers like her—is an example of how God moves in our lives. God is always present, though often unseen and taken for granted. He always believes in his children and wants them to succeed in life, to be happy, and to make a positive difference in the world. Just like my mom.

Thanks, Mom.

And thanks to all the mothers who have given us an understanding of the bottomless depths of God's heart.

———

I also want to thank my wife, Linda, for the example she sets as a godly mother and for her extra support of this project. Thanks for taking care of all the daily chores so that I could concentrate on the work. I never would have made it without your help. All my love is yours.

To my special friend and mentor, Cecil (Cec) Murphey, I find once again I am indebted to your generosity and kindness. Thanks for your hard work and editorial insights.

Bob Hostetler, Michael Brewer, and Bob Mahaffey have all been instrumental and influential in my life. Thank you.

Steve Laube, Julie Smith, and the many laborers at Bethany House have once again made this an enjoyable endeavor. I appreciate all the things you do, seen and unseen, to make my job easier.

Special thanks to Karen Solem and Spencerhill Associates, Ltd.

My computer expert and brother, Walter Holmes, kept me going when the computer went dead. Thank you for your technical support, but also for your moral support. Thanks as well to my older brother, Fred Randall Holmes, who has always given encouragement and leadership.

Finally, to all the writers whose words appear in this book, thank you for sharing your stories. May your words touch many lives and draw us closer to the heart of God.

CONTENTS

SECTION FOUR:

🐑 THE GRACE OF A MOTHER 🐑

SECTION FIVE:

🐑 THE COMFORT OF A MOTHER 🐑

SECTION SIX:

🐑 THE STRENGTH OF A MOTHER 🐑

SECTION SEVEN:

❦ THE LESSONS OF A MOTHER ❦

SECTION EIGHT:

❦ THE PROVISION OF A MOTHER ❦

SECTION NINE:

❦ THE PRESENCE OF A MOTHER ❦

SECTION TEN:

🐦 THE UNCONDITIONAL LOVE OF A MOTHER 🐦

INTRODUCTION

I don't remember when I didn't love Jesus," Shirley Murphey said to her Sunday school class. "From the day I was born my mother talked to me constantly about the Savior. The first word I ever spoke was *Jesus*. But it was more than her talking about him or teaching me. My mother lived the kind of life that made me want to love Jesus."

Some mothers are like that.

Not surprisingly, godly mothers are a major force in the spiritual development of their children. They take their children to church. They sing songs about God's love. They spend time in prayer. Most important, they demonstrate a life of faith.

Mothers lift us up when we are down. They cheer us on when we are discouraged. They pitch in and help whenever they see a need.

If we want to understand God's heart, and find ways of drawing close to him, a good place to look would be at the lives of mothers who have given us glimpses of God's love by their everyday deeds of service.

Abraham Lincoln once said, "No one is poor who had a godly mother."

These true stories are about mothers who have made our world a richer place.

SECTION *One*

The WISDOM
OF A MOTHER

I WOULD GIVE MY CHILD THE GIFT OF FRIENDSHIP

GLORIA GAITHER, PEGGY BENSON, SUE BUCHANAN, JOY MACKENZIE

from *Confessions of Four Friends Through Thick and Thin*

GLORIA GAITHER

I would give my children the gift of friendship. I would have them know the joy of sharing their hearts without having to speak words, to know they're forgiven without having to ask forgiveness, to know they are valued without having to achieve.

I would have them know the assurance of a clasped hand, the meaning of an exchanged glance, the stirring of a shared joy, the empathy of an unexpressed disappointment.

I want them to grow up surrounded by the honest exchange of ideas and opinions, the risking of new experiences and adventures, the delight in enjoying the simple things, a circle of familiar friends. This will help them know that friendships are necessary, possible, and worth the struggle that all great relationships demand.

I would have my children experience and enjoy friendships that cross age, race, gender, cultural, and religious lines—friendships that grow because they're nurtured, thrive because they're valued, and survive because they're resilient. I would like our circle of friends to be the kind that would help our children prepare the soil of their hearts for the seeds of friendship and help them learn to care for the tender sprouts of friendships in their young lives.

I would like our home to be a place where friendships can grow, blossom, and mature—a garden of friendship where strong-rooted, deep, old friendships thrive alongside new, experimental ones, hardy ones with fragile ones that need a lot of care.

I would teach our children that the greatest Friend of all is the God of the Universe, who cared so much about relationships that He chose to walk the dusty roads of earth with us. He confined His great mind to our finite thoughts and expressed His unfathomable truths in the words of a human language. He exchanged the grandeur of heaven for a simple carpenter's home, a friend's guest room, and a borrowed tomb. And He traded having us all as His slaves and servants for enjoying us as His friends.

Most important of all, I would have my children know the great joy of an honest and intimate relationship with the Friend who sticks closer than a brother or sister.

————

In the garden of friendship, stained knees, dirt beneath the nails, unsightly messes—the unpretty—are welcomed. We are on amiable terms with heat and cold and mud and dust. No need to be concerned with looks or outward appearances among friends. This is the potting shed where problems are solved and life is nourished, rearranged, rejuvenated.

THE CASSETTE TAPE

BETH MOORE

from *Feathers From My Nest: A Mother's Reflections*

When our children were little, Keith and I were sure we had them pegged. Like lots of parents, we stereotyped them from the start. "Amanda is a carbon copy of her mother, and Melissa is a carbon copy of her father," we used to say. Translation: Amanda was (1) afraid of her shadow and (2) very diplomatic in her relationships. Melissa was (1) frightfully deficient of healthy fear and (2) never had a thought she didn't vocalize. Yep. One was her mother. The other was her father. We knew what to expect. Case closed. Then they had the nerve to squirm right out of that "case" and start breaking the genetic rules. While still maintaining much of her mom's take on life, Amanda began developing far more of her daddy's reserve and his preference for smaller, more intimate groups of people. The waters of her soul run deep, and she's a wonderful listener whose favorite ministry style so far is one-on-one, much like her father. Melissa, a delightful Daddy's girl, staggered her father's imagination when she developed a love for scads of people and could make a new best friend in five seconds flat. She is willing to share whatever she's learned (and a few things she hasn't) with whomever will listen, much like her mama. But you'd better be ready to hear what she really thinks because, like her daddy, she still has a rare thought she doesn't lend considerable volume.

Both our girls have turned out to be interesting concoctions of the two most diverse people the Lord Jesus may ever have pronounced man and wife. If either girl finds herself on a psychiatrist's couch one of these days complaining of an unexplainable sense of inner conflict, I can explain it: The parts of Keith and me inside of them are having a fight. And I'm sorry. I'm sure he is, too, but he'll save his admissions for a smaller, more intimate group of people. I'll just go ahead and tell everyone who will listen. All I know to tell my daughters is that their father and I not only learned to get along; we eventually became one another's biggest fans. "Just wait ten or fifteen years, girls, and everyone inside of you will start liking each other much better. You'll see. Until then, there's gonna be a war in there."

As free as Melissa has been with her art of expression, when she was about ten years old, I happened on proof that she really *did* have the ability to hold her tongue if absolutely necessary. Like, for instance, in matters of life and death. In the old days, I used to record cassette tapes of various high-energy Christian contemporary songs I owned so that I could listen to them for motivation while I exercised. The kids loved the tapes, too, and I often had to fish them out of their rooms. One day while I was putting clean clothes away, I found an old favorite tape stuck way back in one of Melissa's drawers. I couldn't wait to pull on my sweats, grab my hand weights, throw that tape in my player, and head out the door for a vigorous walk. I pitched the clean clothes and took to the street.

It was a blast. The weather was crisp and beautiful and the music was sublime. I turned the volume up as loud as I could stand. The words to the songs filled my soul, and I sang right with them at the top of my lungs. Too bad my neighbors couldn't hear the accompaniment. I've been known to put both my weights in one hand so that I can lift up the other in praise while I'm on my walks. Sometimes the neighbors make their children come inside until Mrs. Moore passes by. The day I found the old tape was one of those days when they would have shut the mini-blinds.

I was caught up in praise and worship, pumping six pounds of iron to beat the band, and making a joyful noise, when all at once the music on my home-made tape was interrupted by a terrible racket. The noise had the familiar ring of a novice trying to make a recording. I listened carefully as it became clearer and clearer that someone had recorded over my tape right in the middle of one of the best songs. The tape picked up sounds made by someone fiddling with the buttons on the recorder, then sighs of exasperation, and finally a little voice that said, "There. Now I can get started." I immediately recognized the voice of my youngest daughter. As many things as I had heard her say, nothing could have prepared me for what came next. She commenced to speak her mind on some matters she'd wisely chosen not to pursue with me. My eyes grew as wide as saucers and I stopped dead in my tracks, listening to my ten-year-old give her mother the "once over." She drew a breath and then she gave me the twice over. She had it out with me right there on tape. I can no longer remember what decision I had made with which she begged to differ, but I assure you, she did not mince words. My chin hit the ground as I heard a mouthful of things most kids threaten to say to their parents but prudently resist. I could just see that child standing in the middle of her bed, hands on her hips, "sportin' a proper 'tude" with that head tilting side to side, taking a breath only long enough to say, "And another thing. . . !" Only my Melissa would have recorded her thoughts for future listening pleasure.

Before you think I was terribly appalled, keep in mind this was my second child. Not my first. The truth is, I doubled over and laughed so hard that I had to roll in the grass in one of my neighbor's front yards. She even called her dog in the house. For all I know, she may have wanted to call the police. I would love to have explained my behavior to her, but I had a sneaking suspicion she wouldn't have "gotten" it. From all appearances she hadn't had a good laugh since 1972 and didn't look to be in the mood for a fresh encounter. Picture me saying, "You don't understand! This is my daughter telling me off! It's just hilarious!" Picturing the expression on Melissa's face and what her body language must have been like as she told me off made me laugh so hard I cried. What I would have given to be a bug on that wall when she was making her debut recording! As soon as I could pull myself together, I made a beeline right back to my house with the grass still clinging to my sweats. I called my mom and shared every word of it with her. She laughed her dentures off. I didn't say a word to Melissa about finding the tape for years. I don't doubt, however, that when she got off the school bus that day, I had a very suspicious smirk on my face.

The tape certainly wasn't a punishable offense. She hadn't liked my decision that day she made the recording, but she had obeyed me. I didn't ordinarily demand that my children act ecstatic about decisions they didn't like or understand. I preferred they be respectful, and I certainly expected their obedience, but Keith and I let them voice a measure of their displeasure if we could see they needed to be heard. I feel like God's that way with us at times. I don't always like His decisions, but when I choose to obey Him, the act of obedience still "counts" with Him even if I'm not thrilled about it. On occasion I feel like God has said to me, "Kick and scream all you want. Go right ahead and have a fit. Then when you're finished, do what I've asked you to do." Sometimes I said the same thing to my children.

Melissa talked big, but she almost always ended up doing what I asked. I remember a few times when I had to respond with a no to something she desperately wanted to do and she threatened, "What if I do it anyway?" I am so grateful that she was the kind of child I could answer like this: "Baby, you won't. Because even though you're mad at me and you don't like my decision, you are a child who obeys her parents, and I have confidence that you will do what we've asked." Sometimes I'd hold my breath and pray my head off, but she rarely let me down. She'd kick and scream and have a fit, but in the end she almost always did the right thing.

I happen to think God's not terribly offended when we do something similar. The last thing I'm recommending is telling God off, but I don't think an occasional fit under dreadfully strenuous circumstances is terminal. I'm not talking about a tantrum lifestyle. We'd be little more than childish brats. I'm talking about those times when we want God to move in a certain way or grant us something so badly we can hardly bear it, and He simply and emphatically says no. Something important to us. Maybe even a matter of life and death concerning someone we love. Or maybe what we want is something He granted to "so and so" but has withheld from us. Sound familiar? That can be as frustrating to us as it is to our children when their friends get things they don't. We can be so devastated over a divine ruling that we want to throw a fit. At the risk of sounding like a heretic, I'd like ever so gently to suggest that we might consider having one. It sure beats shutting down spiritually or turning our backs on the things of the faith. Since there's no way to have a fit behind God's back, I believe He'd just as soon we throw it right there in front of Him, dumping our frustrations and disappointments right into His lap.

THE DAY MAMA
BAKED THE BIRD

CLINT KELLY

One balmy Thanksgiving Day in Southern California, our kitchen was alive with preparations for the annual feast. Mama was preparing an ostrich-sized Butterball turkey, Dad was setting up the backyard eatery for an army of relatives, and my eleven-year-old growling stomach and I were trying to stay out of everyone's way.

Coming back from the neighborhood park where I'd gone to play, a bright river of sound washed up and down the block. Sunkist, my orange German roller canary, was in his cage on the front porch table singing an aria of joy for the entire world to hear.

I loved that sound. Struggling as I was in those days to control a bad temper, it was the one sound guaranteed to put me in a better mood.

In the kitchen, Mom playfully smacked my hands away from the jellied cranberries and stood good-natured guard over the sweet pickles. We sang two stanzas of "The Battle Hymn of the Republic" and were just launching into a third when the crash came.

My eyes locked with Mom's and instantly we recognized the sound. The front porch was not enclosed and the neighbor's cat—never before a problem—must have decided to get a bird of its own for Thanksgiving.

The cage was flat on its side, door ajar. Sunkist, still as one of those artificial birds in a floral arrangement, was on his back, feet stiffly curled, tiny eyes shut tight.

Like hot lava, anger welled up inside me. Tears threatened to fall.

I looked wildly about for the cat, murder on my mind.

Mama went straight for the canary.

"Not to worry," she chirped. "Mine eyes have seen the glory!"

With that, she scooped Sunkist into the palm of her hand and gently took him inside the house.

Curiosity overcame my "mad" and I trailed after her.

Back in the fragrant kitchen, Mom did the most astonishing thing. She slid Sunkist carefully into a brown paper lunch sack, set the bag and its feathered contents into the oven, left the door ajar, and turned the oven to 250 degrees.

I looked at my mother in panic. I stared at the naked turkey still sitting on the counter in its roasting pan. I gazed fearfully at the bag of canary in the oven. In that instant I knew the awful truth. Mama, in her grief, had snapped. She had confused the birds.

We were going to have baked canary for Thanksgiving.

She looked strangely calm. "Just you wait," she said, and added a wink. "Just you wait."

I waited for what seemed an eternity. A kidney transplant didn't take as long. And then I heard it.

Che-ep . . . Cheep . . . CHEEP!

Each cheep was stronger than the one before.

The bag on the oven grate began to rustle and rock.

Mom winked again. "Bird's done!" she sang, handing me the lunch sack, warm from the oven.

"Wha-what?" I stammered.

Mama laughed and then assumed her wisest expression. "Always keep shock victims warm," she said with exaggerated authority, as if she were the Surgeon General.

Gingerly, I parted the top of the bag and peered down upon a very indignant canary peering up. Stern eye cocked, orange feathers ruffled, he seemed to demand, "Just what is the meaning of this? Would you stick Pavarotti in a bag?"

Mama and I put Sunkist back in his cage and set it safely inside the house by a sunny kitchen window. He began to sing with renewed gusto. I put my arms around Mama and held on for a long time, saying nothing. She started to hum. "Mine eyes have seen the glory . . ."

I squeezed her. She squeezed me. We burst out laughing. My anger evaporated.

23

How many of us, when faced with an assault on what we hold most dear, react like I did right after the crash?

I wanted to kill the cat.

Mama cradled the canary.

God is a cradler, a Redeemer of lost causes, not a seeker of retribution. Jesus gave His life for the fallen sparrows. The heart of a godly mother knows these things.

THE CANDY BAR WARS

DOUGLAS KNOX

One of the greatest memories from my youth is the way my mother was able to draw moral lessons from daily occurrences. With measured words she would take my brother, sister, or me aside and walk us through a patient explanation about something we had done, taking pains to make sure we understood the moral at the end of the story.

That was on our good days. On the bad days we learned at the end of a board, with measured swing.

The most difficult lesson I ever had to learn didn't come at the end of a board. It happened when I lost the last battle of the Candy Bar Wars.

My sister, Beth, was still a baby, leaving my brother Mark and me to be the operative members of the Knox kids. Older by three and a half years, I was the undisputed Alpha male. It was a role that I took seriously.

The afternoon began simply enough. Mom and Dad asked the neighbor to watch us while they did their weekly grocery shopping. When they came back home, however, we discovered that they had brought us a candy bar. A single candy bar. Mom set it on the counter and told us that after supper we could share it.

It was a Three Musketeers bar. The television commercials had rehearsed the candy's wonders until we had them memorized—thick chocolate nougat in the middle, drenched in creamy milk chocolate.

We were delighted. Candy bars were a rare treat, and even half a bar was better than nothing.

Every time we stole into the kitchen we gazed at the coveted delicacy. The mere sight gave us shivers of euphoria—and elicited a realization as primal as sinful human nature. One of us would have to settle for a smaller piece than the other.

Never mind the fact that Mom's cutting eye was so sharp we'd both have to scrutinize the pieces to decide which was larger. The difference mattered more than the gift.

We talked about our treat in conspiratorial voices throughout the afternoon, believing that as long as we kept the other thinking about the delights of the Three Musketeers bar he would miss the real issue. The one who got to choose first would get the bigger piece.

In my mind, the case was clear. I was the older/bigger/stronger brother. The bigger piece was mine by birthright. I'm sure Mark was equally convinced that as the younger/smaller/less-privileged brother, he was the one who deserved first choice.

Jealousy reigned in our minds. The constant thought that one of us would walk away with an ever-so-slightly bigger piece raised the ante to astronomical proportions. Mark and I were screaming for first choice before Mom removed the wrapper.

Mom's patience snapped. She slammed the candy bar on the wooden cutting board, thrust the knife handle at me, and then pointed at Mark. "That's it!" she yelled. "You cut it, and you take the first piece."

I took the knife, horrified. I didn't know where the halfway mark was. My treat would end up lopsided if I cut it, and that would be less fair than anything Mom would have done.

I begged for clemency. Didn't Mom know that I'd tried to cut a grapefruit in half once, and it ended up with a piece that looked like I'd spooned it out of the other? Why couldn't Mom make Mark cut the candy bar so I could save face and get the bigger piece?

Mom refused to budge.

Mark watched me with a smug grin.

I laid the knife on the creamy milk chocolate topping and tried to deal with the sensory overload. Both sides had to be equal. The knife had to be perfectly vertical and straight. Check and recheck everything, and then center the knife again. Too much rode on this to make a mistake.

I made the cut.

The Three Musketeers bar split down a sloping diagonal, leaving one piece at least a full bite larger than the other. Before I could break myself from the horror of my lopsided hack job, Mark dove for the larger piece.

I howled in protest.

Mom told me to take my piece or give it up altogether. I skulked away and ate my less-than-half of the Three Musketeers in shame.

I lost two battles that evening. First I failed to dissuade Mom from her judgment. Then, like the older Esau before Jacob, I had to capitulate to my younger brother.

After the double humiliation, I walked away with a valuable nugget of truth. It was better not to split hairs when it came time for Mom to split candy bars.

––––––––

That incident is almost forty-five years distant now, and Mark and I laugh about it every time we get together. Mark often says, "The wisdom of Solomon." He's right. Mom showed incredible fortitude that evening. If she had given in, she would have missed an opportunity to teach me a valuable life lesson.

I finally picked up on the bigger picture, the one that Mom worked so hard to get us to see. Fairness day in and day out is fiction. Those who strive for it, as Solomon wrote, only grasp at the wind. How much better is it to think about the needs of others first and to delight in their good fortune.

I'VE DISCOVERED THE BENEFITS OF BITING MY TONGUE

GLORIA GAITHER,
PEGGY BENSON,
SUE BUCHANAN,
JOY MACKENZIE

from *Confessions of Four Friends Through Thick and Thin*

SUE BUCHANAN

From the time Dana was born, we prayed that she would someday marry the right person and that it would be God's choice, not ours. It took Dana a long time to show even the slightest interest in boys. She was a late bloomer. By the time she was in the eleventh grade, we'd pretty much pegged her as antisocial and slightly boring. Yes, I know she is my very own daughter and that's a cruel thing to say, but sometimes a mother has to face facts.

Then in her senior year, she discovered the harp, and suddenly she was known; she was in demand to play at every event: talent shows and musicals—she even became a member of the Nashville Youth Symphony. One night when she returned from a rehearsal—we always waited up to help her unload, lamenting the fact she hadn't chosen to play piccolo—she had with her the cutest, tallest, most muscular, blond-haired boy you ever laid eyes on. Balanced on one shoulder was the harp. Heretofore, it took the three of us to manipulate it out of the station wagon, into the house and up the stairs. *Whoosh,* went the wind out of Wayne's sails when he realized he might never be needed again. If for no other reason than that, we knew this boy couldn't possibly be the one.

After the blond Adonis came a total opposite: a dark, fun-loving Jewish boy, and we all fell in love, especially Wayne after he discovered David couldn't move the harp by himself. My guess is, knowing David, that even if he could have, he was smart enough to play the game.

It wasn't unusual for Dana and David to come home late after a date and barge right in to our room ready to entertain us with their evening's adventures. It was fun while it lasted. We knew down deep David wasn't the one; his background was very Jewish, and Dana's was very Christian. Each recognized that their heritage was part of who they were, and neither intended to change.

In college Dana met Barry, and it didn't take long for us to figure out this was the one! Watching the two of them together was like watching six-year-olds who simply took delight in each other's presence. Barry's parents, Bonnie and Miles, whom we'd met and fallen in love with, were having the same thoughts we were: these two were meant for each other. In our minds, Bonnie and I were planning a wedding. We chose the colors for our dresses, for heaven's sake!

The problem was that Dana and Barry didn't cooperate! Dana assured us they could never date; they were best friends. "Almost like brothers and sisters," she said. They graduated from college with no wedding in sight.

Every year, Dana and Barry and their other best friends, Deba and Cary (also not a couple), took a vacation together. Throughout the year, they would visit each other: Barry would come to Nashville, or she would go to Middletown, Ohio. They dated other people, and if he broke up with someone, she was by his side, comforting him. If she broke up with someone, Barry was there, hugging, patting, consoling.

Looked like love to me, but what do I know? I'm just the mother. Once when I was planning a business trip to Columbus, Ohio, Dana insisted that instead of flying I should drive so she could go with me. The plan would be to drop her off in Middletown on the way and pick her up on the way back. Things went according to plan. I dropped her off, continued to Columbus for a couple of days, did my work, and returned to the designated meeting place in Middletown: the Bob Evans restaurant. They were there, and I pulled in next to them. And I waited. I waited and waited and waited!

When I glanced their way, I could see they were in heavy conversation. I waited!

Even though I tried to keep my glances at a minimum, I couldn't help but notice after a while that Dana was becoming more and more animated. Not in a good way. I knew my daughter well, and I recognized not in a good way when I saw it. I waited!

For forty-five minutes I waited, and at last Dana jumped out, slammed the door, threw her duffle bag in the back seat of my car, slammed the door, jumped in my car, and slammed the door.

"Go!" she ordered. "Go!" She didn't look back. She didn't wave. And there was certainly no sisterly kiss blown through the breeze, the kind you would expect to see when best friends part.

The look on her face was the look you save for someone who has killed your pet parakeet. She was steaming! Smoke was coming out her nostrils.

I bit my tongue!

"The nerve of him," she said. "You'll never believe it! You will *ne-ver in a million years* believe it!"

I bit my tongue.

"Mother, I am so mad!" she said. "He loves me." It was like she'd just been proposed to by the Ayatollah! She slapped the dashboard for punctuation.

I bit my tongue.

"He's loved me for years. Can you believe it?"

I bit my tongue.

"Know what he said? He said he wants to get married but he can't wait for me forever." She slapped the dashboard.

"He says he'll have to find someone else if I won't marry him. Can you believe that?" Another slap on the dashboard.

I bit my tongue.

" 'Of course, find someone!' I told him. 'Of course, get married! We're just best friends. Always were, always will be.' "

There was quiet for a moment, followed by another slap on the dashboard. I noticed that her poor hand was bright red from the trauma.

As for me, I was thinking I could taste blood running down my throat as a result of my tongue biting! I wondered if the emergency room in the next town was equipped to handle severe carpal tunnel syndrome and tongue biting trauma.

"I'll tell you one thing, though," she said, eyes flashing. The dashboard punctuation was now coming with every word she expelled. "Whoever he marries better understand our relationship!"

I could contain myself no longer. I burst out laughing. I'd just taken a mouthful of iced tea, and I spewed it all over me, the dashboard, and the windshield.

"What?" she screeched like a banshee, her face now between me and the road, presenting another problem that might end in the trauma center.

"I can promise you," I said, "whoever he marries won't understand the relationship."

It was quiet the rest of the way home.

The friendship somehow continued—unchanged as far as I could tell. In the fall, Dana told us that Barry had a girlfriend. In October she asked us if we could get a ticket for the girl for Praise Gathering. We agreed, and Dana made arrangements for us to meet up with her at our hotel. Just before we left for Indianapolis, Dana phoned.

"Call me as soon as you meet her, and tell me what she's like. Barry Shafer deserves the best. In fact, he deserves perfect. This girl needs to be perfect."

Somehow our plans for meeting went awry and we never laid eyes on the girl; we left her ticket at the desk. When we arrived home, Dana was on our doorstep.

"So what's she like? Is she witty, and clever? And fun? Barry's the funnest person in the world. He needs somebody fun. Does she love the Lord? Nobody loves the Lord more than Barry Shafer. Is she cute? Is she pretty? Is she right for Barry?" Wayne and I were ready!

"Oh, I don't know," I said, taking my time. "I guess you could say she's . . . (I'm milking it for all it's worth) . . . she's cuddly." Wayne shook his head in agreement.

"*Cuddly?* CUDDLY?" Dana screeched, eyes flashing. "She's *cuddly?* What kind of a person is that?"

The next event in the saga of Dana and Barry was a ski trip by the same faithful foursome, followed the very next weekend by a visit by Barry to

Nashville. That surprised me, since they'd just been together, but as usual we planned a big family dinner.

After the meal as we sat around the living room, I noticed that Dana was sitting on the floor by Barry's chair. Was I mistaken, or was she leaning against his leg? Was I mistaken, or was she looking at him like he was Tom Cruise? Was I mistaken, or every time he opened his mouth was she confusing him with Billy Graham? Then the clincher! He reached out and stroked her hair! This in itself could be the eighth wonder of the world, because Dana cannot stand to have her hair touched. From the time she was a small child, her hair was off limits. I always blamed it on the fact that she had such heavy hair, it actually gave her pain to have it messed with. Whatever the reason, you just didn't go there. But Barry was going there! And she was behaving like a dopey little kitten. She was loving it! She was all but purring!

Later, we pieced together the story. She had turned around on the ski slopes to see him skiing toward her, and her heart leaped out of her body. She threw him down right there in the snow, did heaven knows what (a mother doesn't want to know!), and the rest is history.

Like I said, when it comes to your children, you should just bite your tongue and pray (knowing in your heart you have the answers). I just don't always take my own advice.

TEACHING GRANDMA

JEAN DAVIS

Grandmothers don't know everything. At least I don't, but I'm smart enough to learn from my children.

When our granddaughter Kayla was almost three, she and her mother, Libby, lived with us. While Libby, a single mom, went to school as a full-time student and worked two jobs, I got to enjoy spending my days playing Grandma.

While Libby was gone, Kayla and I baked cookies. She helped me wash dishes and fold clothes. We cleaned together and bought groceries. We went to the library to get stacks and stacks of books to read. But always in our activities we thought of her mommie. "These are Mommie's favorite cookies. She'll like these," or "Let's get this book for Mommie. She'll love this one about kitties."

After Libby left for school early one June morning, Kayla and I went to a garden center where she helped me choose bedding plants for our flower beds. Later as we set out the plants, I dug the hole, Kayla set each plant in place, and together we patted down the soil around the root ball. While we admired our work of reds, pinks, whites, and yellows, Kayla took off her gardening gloves. We had a few plants left over. "Kayla," I said, "let's surprise Mommie. Let's put this plant in a flowerpot for her. She can keep it in her room." Kayla squealed with delight.

We took our project indoors. I put newspaper on the table and took in the bag of potting soil. In our dining room Kayla helped me fill the flowerpot with rich, black dirt. Then she set the pink and white foliage in place. "Mommie will love this," I said. Kayla agreed.

It was a long day waiting for Mommie and near dark when Libby finally got in. I had forgotten about the surprise, but Kayla hadn't. I left meat sizzling in the skillet to walk into the living room to talk to Libby. The first thing I saw when I entered the room was black potting soil on my beige sofa. Kayla had spilled the contents of the flowerpot. The next thing I saw was Kayla standing by the sofa and her mother sitting on the sofa by the mess.

I have to admit my first impulse was to say something I'm glad I didn't, something I'd surely regret. Before I had a chance to voice my ire, Kayla's mommie said, "Look, Grandma. See what a nice job Kayla did wrapping my present?" I hadn't noticed the piece of typing paper Kayla had crudely wrapped around the pot until then. Of course, if you are not yet three and you need to wrap a potted plant, what better way to do it than to place the flowerpot on its side?

Tears stung my eyes. I had been ready to pounce because someone had gotten black potting soil on my beige sofa, but thankfully someone's mother was there to see what happened. She saw the heart of her precious daughter; I only saw my precious sofa.

"Yes," I said, swallowing the lump in my throat, finally able to answer in the same quiet tone my daughter had. "You did do a nice job wrapping Mommie's present. Good job, Kayla!"

While Libby hugged Kayla, thanking her for her gift, I scooped up the potting soil and placed it back in the pot to secure the plant. When Libby and Kayla went off together to set the table for supper, I turned the meat in the skillet, then got out the hand vacuum.

The sofa cleaned up. The plant grew, as well as the child. And so did the grandma. I am glad we serve a God who knows us so well that He is able to see our hearts and not just our actions. How He must delight in each of our baby steps, even when we make a mess.

SECTION *two*

The PRAYERS
OF A MOTHER

FERVENT LOVE

PATRICK BORDERS

I'm concerned about your little boy," the doctor said. In the corner of the tiny examining room, my wife, Tonya, cradled Jared. "I believe he has meningitis."

An hour earlier, as our family enjoyed a normal weekday dinner, Tonya noticed our son looking ill. His face was pale and cold, and his rosy lips had turned a disturbing shade of blue.

While Tonya held him, I called the doctor's after-hours number and spoke with a nurse. "Get him to a hospital as soon as you can," she said.

Immediately, we abandoned our dinner and piled into the car. Tonya sat next to Jared, observing him. He fell asleep as we pulled out of the driveway. By the time we arrived at the emergency room, Jared's face had faded to a ghostly white; his lips had darkened to a deeper blue.

Shaking him gently, Tonya tried to wake him. He breathed naturally but didn't respond. "Dear God, what's happening?" she said. Terror was overtaking us.

In the examining room, a nurse came in to draw blood. Jared didn't budge as the needle pricked. Even involuntary movements, like a grimace or flutter of his eyelids, were strangely absent. Tonya wrapped him in her arms like a cocoon; her shoulders bent over him in a protective cover. He looked lifeless.

The diagnosis of meningitis stunned us. "Are you sure?" I asked the doctor.

"He's demonstrating the early symptoms," he said. "We'll need to run some tests to determine what's happening."

For the second time in a year, we faced losing our beautiful child. A preemie at birth, Jared had struggled his first few days until his lungs strengthened. Tonya's devotion to Jared had been immediate and powerful as she filled those days with tears, prayers, and bedside encouragement. Now Tonya rocked Jared as she had then. Tears cascaded down her cheeks. The harsh fluorescent lights

accentuated his colorless appearance. He was deadly still.

"Come on, Jared," she said softly. "It's okay, Little Man. Mama's here." Her eyes strained in agony. "You can snap out of this. You can do it." She bent lower and kissed his forehead.

Nurses continued hustling in and out of the room. Tonya seemed unaware of their activity; her attention was fully concentrated on our precious son.

In a panic, I called our pediatrician at home. As I relayed the situation to him, Tonya continued rocking Jared and began talking quietly. She was praying in her intimate way as if God were sitting with her—a daughter pleading with her father. Tonya and Jared swayed as one.

I hung up the phone. Feeling helpless, I sat down, closed my eyes, and listened.

"Wrap yourself around him, God. Please heal him. Please heal him," she was saying. "Guide the doctor's hands. Help him bring Jared back." She continued repeating her prayer; her compassion seemed to lead her into a deeper presence with God.

Then she stopped talking.

I opened my eyes and stared at her. She still cried, but her eyes were relaxed, peaceful. "He's going to be okay," she stated calmly. She wiped her tears and took a deep breath. "I heard a voice. A very clear voice said, 'The child will be all right.' It was the most peaceful sound I've ever heard."

I said nothing as I tried to absorb what she told me.

"He's going to be all right," she repeated, stroking Jared's cheek. Her voice was clear and strong.

Within minutes the doctor returned, saying Jared required a strong antibiotic and fluids. "In a normal situation, this antibiotic shot causes a great deal of pain," he said. "We'll take good care of him, but we recommend you go into the waiting room while we administer the medication."

"No, I'll stay," Tonya replied.

"The reaction is hard on parents, especially the moms. Even if he doesn't respond, it'll probably be a long night. The break would do you good," he said.

"He'll need me when he wakes. I'll stay," she said firmly. She refused to be separated from our son now. Her maternal love would not allow it.

I doubted the shot would faze Jared; he was still unresponsive to stimulation. Tonya snuggled him to her chest as the nurse prepared the syringe. I watched as she cleaned his leg and inserted the needle and medication into his vein.

Instantly, Jared's eyes rolled back. His lips parted slightly, and he grimaced. I detected a quiet whimper, which grew into a louder whine, then a cry, and finally a scream. His eyes opened in confusion and pain—darting around until they found Tonya's face.

Her soothing fingers combed his blond hair. "There, there," she said. "You're going to be fine."

At any other time, hearing our baby scream would be hard to bear. Now we rejoiced in the sound of life. He screamed for ten more minutes. His cheeks flushed red; pink returned to his lips.

"Thank you," Tonya whispered. She dried his cheeks with a tissue from her pocket, as tears of joy poured down her own face.

Over the next hour Jared was closely observed. He gradually recovered and was soon sitting upright in Tonya's lap, her arms hugging him. He gazed curiously around the room and chewed on crackers Tonya kept in her purse.

"It appears the pain of the shot has broken whatever had hold of him," the doctor said, smiling. "The blood work was inconclusive, but I think it's safe to take him home."

We arrived home elated though shell-shocked. Our cold dinners sat on the table, our normal lives frozen in time. Jared slept in our bed that night with his head nestled between Tonya's chest and arm. We checked on him constantly; he was always fine. By the next afternoon, he crawled around and played with his sister.

Did Jared acquire a harmless illness, which hit hard and left quickly, or did we witness a miracle? I don't know for sure, but I know I witnessed the fervent love of a mother. During that terrible and wonderful evening in the hospital, Tonya had cared for Jared the way God cared for both of them—the way God cares for all his children.

That happened four years ago. Today Jared is healthy and active. As I think back on Tonya's quiet, tender dedication, it reminds me that mothers are like that. In some ways, they are God's hands on earth—they hold, caress, soothe, and most of all, they feel our pain with us.

LOSING JEFF

LISA HUSSEY

from *Psalms for the Single Mom*

The doorbell rings, and the first trick-or-treater stands expectantly with bag open.

"Oh, my," I exclaim. "What do we have here?" I shovel handfuls of candy into each waiting sack, smile, and wave at the parents standing guard protectively at the curb. I close my door with a sigh.

Halloween would forever remind me of the day I almost lost Jeff.

We were at Sean's soccer game—one of the hundreds we'd been to at the same park, Wildhorse Creek. It was a sunny autumn day, and I was enjoying talking to the many parents I knew from teaching their children and from my boys' soccer teams.

I kept a watchful eye out for Neil and Jeff, playing behind me on the climbing wall, the tires, and racing up and down the barren hill with the other brothers and sisters of players and collecting the good Georgia red clay as laundry challenges to their moms. Several times, Jeff came running up to tell me something or to ask for a drink of water.

And each time someone would tell me how cute he was.

He was cute, even though it wore thin on me when he tried to use it to get what he wanted.

But it was his coloring—rosy-cheeked, big brown eyes, blond hair—along with his chunky build (Fireplug, I called him), and his funny personality—so animated and excited, lisping all his s's—that really grabbed people and won him fans.

The game ended, the drinks were being passed out, Sean came over to ask me what I thought of his kicks.

I spotted Neil and motioned him over.

I shielded my eyes to look for Jeff.

"Where's Jeff?" I asked Neil lightly when he ran up.

"I dunno," he answered with a shrug.

I turned my head, looking at the perimeter of pine trees surrounding the soccer fields.

"Go check the bathroom," I asked Neil.

"Sean, run up to the concession stand, and if Jeff is there, tell him to come back here!" I shouted.

Several of the parents turned their heads.

"Jeff?" they asked. "I just saw him . . ."

More parents began looking around them, calmly, nonchalantly.

"Nope, Mom, not in the bathroom," reported Neil.

"Hey! Jeff's not at the concession stand, Mom!" yelled Sean.

In the blink of an eye, the mood changed.

The Crosses, Sean's coach and his wife, looked significantly at one another.

Diane, the wife, said, "I'll go over to the horse ring and see if he wandered up there."

Bobby, the coach, said, "I'll take Amanda and see if he's up at the far playground."

Sean called to some of his soccer buddies, "Hey, can you help me look for my little brother in the woods?"

Neil stood, frozen to his spot, and slowly, slowly looked up at me.

I tried to reveal on my face none of the wild thoughts running in my brain.

I don't know how successful I was. Not very, I think.

Soon the woods and the surrounding areas were ringing with "JEFF, JEEEEFFFFF," and I began to relive every moment of what had started out as an ordinary Saturday morning.

I remembered waking him up and smelling that distinctly "Jeff smell"—the sleepy essence that clings to each of my boy's sheets after they've been in them awhile.

I remembered kissing his soft, plump cheeks, and his enormous eyes opening up.

He always wakes up so happy, in contrast to Sean, who wakes up slowly, like me, and Neil, who often wakes up in a blue funk.

When did he disappear? Why didn't I watch him more closely?

Just *who all* had said he was so cute?

Some of those people I didn't even know, and looking around now, I didn't see them anywhere.

My mind's voice said the unthinkable: "Maybe someone took him."

I looked at my watch and realized the game had been over almost an hour. Suddenly, half-remembered snatches of made-for-TV movies came tumbling through my brain.

"In half an hour, your child could be in the next county."

"If you don't find your child in the first hour, the chances are slim to none he or she will ever be recovered alive . . ."

Tears, the first I'd allowed, filled my eyes.

I turned to another mom from the soccer team and asked, "How long do you wait before calling the police?" as calmly as I would have asked what degree oven and how many minutes when learning a new recipe.

Her eyes filled with tears more quickly than mine had.

She grabbed me in a fierce hug and hoarsely whispered, "Bless your heart," into my shaking ear.

The dam broke.

Torrents of tears streamed down my face.

My shoulders shook.

The parents who had returned from their futile searches spoke strength to me with their eyes.

Some shuffled their feet and looked down. I swallowed and, in one instant, got it together.

The crying stopped, the iron will I depended on to get me through crises returned.

But, amazingly, the fervent, steady prayers prayed in strength and peace quickly deteriorated into the bargain-basement variety.

"Please, Lord, let me have my Jeff back," I prayed.

"I promise to be more patient with him when he takes forever to get out of the car.

"I'll never let him out of my sight.

"Let me have one more chance . . ."

And then the cry I'll never forget rang out over that clear October Atlanta air: "WE FOUND HIM!"

"Lisa, we found him! In the woods. Scrunched up. Hiding. He thought he was going to get in trouble, so he didn't answer when he heard us call . . ."

Oh, praise God, they found him.

Never was my son more precious than when I took his scared little face between my shaking hands and said, "Thank You, God! *Thank You,* God!"

His big eyes took in my tears, the crowd around us, the noise, the relief.

And he said, "I'm in BIG trouble, aren't I?"

Suppose one of you has a hundred sheep and loses one of them. Does he not leave the ninety-nine in the open country and go after the lost sheep until he finds it? And when he finds it, he joyfully puts it on his shoulders and goes home. Then he calls his friends and neighbors together and says, "Rejoice with me; I have found my lost sheep" (Luke 15:4).

THE FAITH OF A MOTHER'S PRAYER

TRACIE PETERSON

from *The Eyes of the Heart*

When I was about eight years old, we moved to Dallas, Texas, so that my father could attend computer school for two years. We had never had a lot of money, but moving robbed my folks of what little comfort they'd had. My father's paycheck was much less than it had been, while the bills were every bit as high. On top of this, my folks had acquired new expenses with the move. The budget was tight. The margin for error was zero.

I remember my folks trying to figure out how to make it all come together. We rented a run-down house in a poorer section of town. My mother often joked that the cockroaches helped us move in. My dad said the bugs were big enough to saddle and ride. My sister and I were fairly oblivious to the worries they suffered, because our folks did a good job of hiding their worry from us.

We made soup out of ketchup and called it fun. We bought five-cent bags of week-old bread and considered it a prized find. We filled the deep-fat fryer with water in order to heat a can of black-eyed peas, because my folks couldn't afford both electricity and gas, and the stove was gas operated. I didn't know we had it all that bad, until we went to bed one Saturday evening, and I heard my mother crying from the other room.

Nothing strikes fear in the heart of a child so easily as hearing a parent cry. When parents cry, you know that something really bad has happened. When parents cry, children cry too. And I did.

The next day we ate what was left of the old, dry bread, feeling blessed by the fact that we could toast it. Feeling like kings, because my dad had brought home packets of jelly from work. We went to church not with full bellies, but not empty ones either. Coming home, however, we knew the truth. There was nothing left. There was no food in the house, and payday was five days away.

Eating and playing were my only real concerns at that age. Now one of the major components of my security was missing. The cupboards were bare.

I don't know if this has ever happened to you, but let me tell you, it's a fearful thing. I remember wondering why we couldn't just go to the store and get some food. It seemed very logical to my eight-year-old mind. Never mind the money part.

I was a fairly astute child and saw the worry in my parents' expressions. I'd heard my mother cry the night before. I knew things weren't good, but I didn't know how to help. I asked my mother what we were going to do, and she said, "Pray."

I had known my mother to be a woman of prayer since my first memories of her. She believed in the power of prayer and had great faith that God would see us through. Her faith became food to my soul.

As she began to pray, I felt my spirit calm. I heard her pray for our meal— the meal that wasn't even there. I heard her thank God for the food He would provide. Then she closed the prayer and looked to each of us. "What do we do now?" I asked.

"We wait for God," she told me.

It was only a few minutes later that someone knocked on our front door. In anticipation of answered prayer, I followed my mother and father to the door. Outside, on the front porch, were several of the new friends we'd made at church. Their arms were full with sacks and bundles of food. Not just cans and packages of unprepared food, but also a hot meal, ready for our consumption. Loaves and fishes. Ravens bringing bread and meat.

My mother cried, which made me a bit weepy as well. I wasn't sure why she was crying, and it caused me to fear. Seeing me in such a state, she turned and smiled, saying, "Look what God has provided." The words gave me an over-whelming feeling of confidence in the power of prayer. After our friends left the food and had gone, we sat down to a wonderful lunch, and again my mother praised God for His bounty.

"We are sharing a meal of answered prayer," my mother told us.

The thought intrigued me and forever changed my life. Suddenly every Bible story miracle was visible on my table. God sending manna to the Israelites.

The boy with his fish and bread lunch being multiplied to thousands. Elijah being fed by the ravens. Every single time God had heard the prayers of the destitute was evidenced in that meal. And even at eight years old, I knew the truth of the power of prayer.

A MOTHER'S PRAYER

RACHEL WALLACE-OBERLE

One hot summer afternoon several years ago, my children, Barrett and Thomas, who were nine and six at the time, decided to go biking with a friend. I told them to be careful, and off they rushed, shouting lots of good-byes and I-love-you's. I was busy with various things and gradually became aware they had been gone for a long time, which was unusual; we live in a small town, and bike rides for the boys usually lasted fifteen or twenty minutes. I had no way of knowing where they were.

I began to worry, stories of child abductions filling my head. I had never felt so helpless. Then God seemed to say, "Pray." In my fretful state I was incapable of formulating anything flowery; I just paced and whispered over and over, "Oh, Lord, please put your angels around them. Please bring them home safely."

But as the hours passed, my panic grew. My hands shook. My stomach cramped. Irrational snapshots of funerals and a future without my children loomed before me. The need to throw myself into my Father's arms was overwhelming. I kneeled at the living room couch and poured out my anguish. "Where are they, God?" I cried in desperation.

I clung to him, and within that haven of comfort reserved especially for mothers, he wrapped a blanket of peace around me. Its warmth steadied and soothed my trembling. My thoughts cleared. Somehow, still praying, I managed to make it through the afternoon. As the dinner hour approached, the phone rang. I grabbed it. "Hi, Mom," Barrett said in a small voice.

"Where are you?" I asked, weak with relief.

"We're at Grammie's house," he said.

"No, you're not!" I exclaimed in disbelief. Grammie lives in the city of Waterloo, which is about twenty minutes away. The highway from our town into Waterloo is one of the busiest in the region.

"Yes, we are," Barrett said and began to cry.

I went to get them, and when I heard all about their adventure, the urgency to pray took on new significance. The three of them had bicycled almost half-way into Waterloo; Barrett and Thomas knew this was too far to go, but it was a beautiful day and the rules were temporarily disregarded. At this point, their friend remembered he had a newspaper route to take care of and rushed off toward home. Barrett and Thomas lagged behind, lost their bearings, and had no idea how to get home. They decided the only thing they could do was go on to the city and find Grammie's house; Barrett was sure he knew the way.

The two of them headed down Highway 85, which is notorious for speeding drivers, traffic congestion, and accidents. They stopped at a mall and went in to fill their water bottles and use the washroom. By now rush hour had started. Passing several on and off ramps to the expressway, they negotiated numerous sets of traffic lights and busy intersections before proceeding down the main street. After pedaling down side streets and up a hill, they finally ended up at Grammie's house. She was getting into her car to leave for work as the boys appeared, exhausted and sweating, in her driveway.

"Does your mother know you're here?" she asked in astonishment.

They both shook their heads. The enormity of what they had just done settled upon them. Tears rolled down Barrett's grimy face.

"One more second and I wouldn't have been here, darlings," Grammie said as she hugged them. "What would you have done?"

"We would have turned around and gone home again," Barrett blubbered.

A little later, on the way home, I told the boys that God had instructed me to pray for them. And I hadn't stopped until the phone rang.

Barrett looked at me in awe and said, "After we filled up our water bottles and were on our way to Grammie's, something kept telling me to hurry. I kept hearing it over and over again in my head, 'Hurry, hurry, hurry.' "

"Do you know what that was?" I asked him.

He nodded. "It was God."

Thomas, who was listening intently, piped up, "I was hurrying too." It was the first time he had spoken since my arrival. When Grammie kissed him good-bye, he had held on to me tightly without saying a word.

Wide-eyed, the boys watched the scenery pass as we drove home. They sat close together, small and silent, as their bikes banged and rattled in the trunk.

Barrett has never forgotten the sound of God's voice that day or the power of a mother's prayers. The experience, I am sure, will stay with him for the rest of his life as shining, vivid proof that God is real and prayer works.

I REALIZE I'VE BEEN PRAYING WRONG MY WHOLE LIFE

SUE BUCHANAN, JOY MACKENZIE, GLORIA GAITHER, PEGGY BENSON

from *Confessions of Four Friends Through Thick and Thin*

SUE BUCHANAN

W ayne and I began to pray for our babies before they were born. It felt rather silly at first, praying for a little blob that made my tummy stick out. Mostly we prayed that "it" would be healthy. And happy, of course! Perhaps Wayne prayed that "it" would be a boy; I've read that most men hope for a boy the first time around. But after about thirty seconds of holding Dana in his arms, he was silly in love and was ready for a house full of girls.

Soon after each of our daughters was born, we were part of a sacred service in our church committing them to God. Kind of a promise to do our part to raise them in a spiritual environment and an acknowledgment that God had our permission to do His part. The congregation was then asked to raise hands promising to support us in our efforts and to pray for us. And just as the congregants had their hands in the air, past the point of no return (and this happens somewhere in the world every Sunday in churches of every persuasion when a baby is baptized or dedicated, as the case may be), the pastor added, "and not just to pray but also to willingly work in the church nursery." Sometimes you can almost hear the screech of brakes as hands jerk to a halt. The next time you are in such a service, note the smug look on the minister's countenance after he pulls off this coup.

When our girls began to walk, we prayed that they would be safe, that they wouldn't ride their little tricycles into the street and be hit by a car, that they wouldn't fall from the top of the slide. And we prayed that they would be happy.

I beseeched God often that He not let my persistent nightmare come true, the one in which the girls and I were stalled on a railroad crossing and a train was coming toward us full speed. As I prayed that prayer, I would rehearse my dream, how I dove over the seat, grabbed them, and frantically ran to safety, where we watched the car become an inferno. Sometimes I got the car started in the nick of time, so in the nick of time that I felt the car shudder from the draft of the train missing my rear bumper by inches. Either outcome caused me to wake up in a sweat.

My mother, not knowing about my dream (I've never told a soul until now), said to me one day, "The things you anticipate in life, the things you worry about, almost never happen. The things that do happen, you couldn't have planned for." That helped! It also helped to be one of the first families in town to buy a small car—a Mustang. In my dream, I could reach the girls more easily. There was another advantage to a small car. It put them in swatting range when they sassed me or fought each other!

You know exactly what I prayed as the girls entered their teenage years! If you are a mother, you've memorized the script. Don't let her get killed in a car wreck. Don't let her hang out with the wrong crowd. Don't let her be attracted to the wrong boy. Don't let her get pregnant. Help her be interested in her schoolwork. Don't let her fail algebra. And puh-leeze, God, let her be happy.

When they were in college, and afterward, I quit giving God specific orders: "Dear God, I have no earthly idea what's going on with my daughter right now, but You do. It's in Your hands." Then, just in case I couldn't trust Him, I had to add, "Just don't let anything happen to her. And for heaven's sake, let her be happy."

I never failed to pray the happy part. And I always pointed out to the girls what would make them happy, like hanging out with the right people, going to church, eating properly, getting enough rest—the list goes on. And if you talked to either of my daughters about this, they would say that I added to the list the things that would make me happy: cleaning their rooms, helping with chores, pulling their hair out of their eyes, wearing the cutey dresses I'd bought instead of jeans. They would describe a sort of "if mama's happy, everybody's happy" lifestyle. Works for me!

Not long ago, we—Dana and her husband, Barry, Mindy, Wayne, and I— sat peacefully at the breakfast table long after the coffee had grown cold, each of us aware, I'm sure, of the years when we rarely sat peacefully together. It suddenly occurred to me that we are happy. This despite the fact that Dana, who is thirty-six, has just been diagnosed with breast cancer and the fact that Mindy is experiencing overwhelming discouragement as she tries to find her way back after years of bad decisions.

"While we are all together," I say, "I want to tell you something important." (This is hard for me to say; I can barely get the words out, but I'm compelled to say it.) "All of your lives I've prayed that you would be happy. This past year I've stopped praying that."

"Thanks a lot!" the girls responded in unison. We laughed.

"My prayer for you is that you'll know God."

It was quiet for a moment, and I thought I saw some puzzled looks. Since then, both of my precious girls have come to me to say thank you and to assure me that my prayer is being answered. Slowly but surely. And my guess would be not in the ways I could have planned or even dreamed.

GROWING PAINS

Growing Pains

SUZY RYAN

Dressed in their best clothes, the line of polished kindergarten kids stood proud, their bulging backpacks slightly drooping their small shoulders. Only their nervous smiles and darting eyes gave away their trepidation at starting the first day of school. I fought back tears, squeezing one last hug from my five-year-old son, Keegan, before his teacher whisked him away to his classroom.

Somewhat dazed, I stumbled to the car, wondering how he could already be starting school. The day dragged, and finally it was time to pick him up. I arrived early, noticing his sigh of relief after spotting me in the crowd of anxious parents.

The precious look on his face was worth every labor pain, every lost hour of sleep, and the endless testing of my patience over the last five years. Before heading home, I found out Keegan had cried during lunchtime. He had clutched his little cooler, refusing to eat anything. That is, until he saw me at 2:30 in the afternoon. Then he devoured his meal!

Day after day this pattern continued, until I thought I couldn't bear it another moment. My heart grieved when I realized he'd lost two of his forty-eight pounds during the first week.

I asked him if he wanted to take a favorite stuffed animal to class. "I only want you, Mom," he quietly replied. I cut a small piece from his special blanket and thrust it in his pocket.

"It's our secret," I explained. "Whenever you're homesick, reach into your pocket, and your blanket will remind you of how much I love you."

"All right, Mom, but pray for me not to feel sad tomorrow."

After dropping Keegan off the next morning, strength seemed to drain from my body. I fought the urge to yank him from school then and there and rush him home to safety.

Instead, I hovered outside the closed classroom door, silently praying:

"Lord, please take care of my little boy and dry his tears. I am trusting you to hold his hand, to guide him. I am relinquishing control of my firstborn son to you."

Starting my prayer, my head felt fuzzy and I wanted to lie down. I couldn't seem to clear my thinking, but I continued asking God for help.

"Most important, dear heavenly Father, will you train him to grow independent of me? You see, God, this is the hard part of my request, because I think I get a sense of security knowing he craves my attention. Please, don't let me become one of those controlling mothers who lives her life through her children. Give me the courage to let him go—to let him grow. Replace the panic in my spirit with joy; joy at being allowed the privilege of experiencing motherhood. Joy knowing I can trust you completely with the child you knew even before he was born." After my prayer, I hurried to my car, leaving the school with a sense of peace for the first time.

Today, just three weeks later, I watch as Keegan sprints toward his classroom with his new friends. My confident, exuberant son, now back to his full forty-eight pounds, has forgotten to say good-bye. I brush away a tear. My son is maturing.

Yes, we are both growing up.

SECTION *Three*

The EXAMPLE OF A MOTHER

TO SOAR AGAIN

LINDA KNIGHT

A glimpse into my mother's hospital room is a glimpse into darkness. The tubes and needles that punctuate her frame hold her in their grasp like a mounted butterfly. Mother will soar no more.

I hate it here. I want to close my eyes and slip away. I want to be home with our three little sons. I want to bake cookies, scrub floors, do laundry, and press this moment away. I want to sear my thoughts into forgetfulness—but no imagining will erase the reality. Death is so close.

I am alone with her now. My father and two brothers have left to get some rest. We have kept vigil for eleven days. I stand beside her bed and touch her hands. I marvel at how fragile they feel, these callused hands that worked so hard for so long, hands that knitted and crocheted and sewed. Hands that baked a thousand apple pies, that picked tomatoes, and steered tractors, and pulled weeds, and planted fields, hands that labored alongside my father for forty-two years.

How quickly life changes. One moment it's a sunny April morning, and the next it's gray and cold, with sirens wailing in the distance, entering your very soul. When the call came that mother was gravely ill, and I opened those steel hospital doors, it was as if I'd entered another world, lit only by the glare of fluorescent lights. One day vanishes into the next, and on it goes.

Mother's clothes lie neatly folded beside her bed, the bright fuchsia sweater she'd knitted just a month ago. Mother's knitting was one reason why so many people admired her. She was always busy knitting something beautiful and then happily giving it away. Her perfectly sewn white slacks lay tucked beneath her sweater. She always was a stickler for a perfect seam.

I have my Bible with me, but I can't open it. It's as if some unseen force is holding me back. This Book whose words have comforted me on many a sleepless night and taught me to trust in the Lord. Suddenly it strikes me how much my mother's hands have been like my Bible.

Finally, I turn to the Twenty-third Psalm and read the words aloud: *"The LORD is my shepherd, I shall not be in want. He makes me lie down in green pastures, he leads me beside quiet waters, he restores my soul."* Mother's eyes show no recognition, and her hands do not stir.

"I'm so sorry." A voice behind me whispers. I turn to see a nurse standing there. She moves quietly to turn off the monitors and gently close my mother's eyes. Then as quietly as she came, she leaves.

So it really is over now. I stroke Mother's cheek and my tears start. I turn to leave, but then blow her a kiss good-bye.

As I exit through the hospital doors, everything feels the same, yet somehow different. Then I catch a glimpse of a beautiful butterfly resting on a flower just outside. I watch as it spreads its wings and flies away. How good of God to let me know—Mother soars again.

MOM, MERS, AND MRS. GRUBB

BOB HOSTETLER

I n many ways, mine was a confusing childhood. A major source of bewilderment was my mother. She was a mystery to me.

It was the late 1960s, and my family was the poorest on the block in a solidly middle-class neighborhood. My friends sported the latest fashions; I wore my brothers' hand-me-downs. Other homes on the block boasted fine furnishings and color televisions; our carpets were threadbare and I was convinced our black-and-white television was old enough to have broadcast John Cameron Swayze reporting the invention of the wheel. Other families parked two cars in their garages; my father worked long hours to keep our '57 Ford Fairlane running, and every day my mother rode the bus an hour each way to her job.

Yet for all our apparent poverty, we were the only family I knew that employed an ironing lady *and* a cleaning woman. In the days before permanent-press, every week my father would take a basket of clothes (which Mom had pre-dampened and rolled up) to a widow everyone called "Mers." She even referred to herself that way—never "Mrs. Mers," just "Mers." She was a long-time member of the Salvation Army church we attended, and exerted tyrannical control over the church kitchen; no one else was permitted even to make coffee, either in her presence or in her absence. She once chased a friend and me out of the kitchen, waving a butcher knife at us and effecting an eerie impression of the farmer's wife in *Three Blind Mice*. To this day I don't know how much—if any—of her threatened violence was an act.

But every week we would drive across town to Mers' tenement apartment, pick up the basket of ironing, and pay her for her work. Once home, Mom took the clothing out, piece by piece, and ironed it again.

"Why do you do that?" one of us would ask from time to time.

"She missed a spot," Mom would say.

"But you do this every time," her questioner would say. "Why do we pay Mers to iron for us if you're just going to do it over?"

Mom would sometimes blush. She must have felt the implied reproach in our words. But she would shrug or smile and say, "Mers needs the money."

It was the same with Mrs. Grubb, our cleaning lady. Another widow living on a limited income, Mrs. Grubb came to our house every week. She was a cheerless woman, who seemed to approach every cleaning task as though we children had created it solely to make her life miserable. And we paid dearly for it. Mrs. Grubb left behind a wake of streaked windows, sticky linoleum floors, and half-dusted surfaces every Thursday. Every Saturday, Mom would put my brothers and me to work correcting Mrs. Grubb's cleaning job.

"Why do you do that?" one of us would ask.

"I don't want people to think we live in a pigsty," she would answer.

"But we wouldn't have to clean so much if we didn't have a cleaning lady," we would say. "Why do you pay her to clean if you're just going to make us do it over again a couple of days later?"

Of course, we knew what the answer would be. "Mrs. Grubb needs the money."

I never understood that. My mom died when I was still a boy, and her relationship with Mers and Mrs. Grubb mystified me for years. Even as I matured into adulthood, I occasionally reflected on my mother's quizzical behavior with a wry smile and a shake of the head. I always suspected that there might have been more to her arrangements with Mers and Mrs. Grubb than I could understand at the time, but I never quite got it. Until just recently.

My son arrived home from school one day and saw Tim, a friend of mine, painting my home office.

"Why is he doing that?" my son asked when we were out of earshot.

I shrugged. "Because I asked him to."

"But you just painted the whole first floor last year!"

The words were out of my mouth before I knew it. "He needs the money," I said.

In that moment, I heard not my own voice, but my mother's. I remembered how often she used such reasoning in reference to Mers and Mrs. Grubb, and the light suddenly dawned in my mind and heart. I realized then that, without my even suspecting it, my mother had taught me how rewarding it can be to secretly give to the needy. She could have told me and my brothers that Jesus commanded us to "give to the needy [without letting] your left hand know what your right hand is doing, so that your giving may be in secret" (Matthew 6:3–4 NIV). But she showed us instead.

It's a lesson I hope my son has learned from me—just as I learned it from my mother.

TIME FOR ONE MORE HAND?

KAY SHOSTAK

Your daddy gets home in thirty minutes. Now help me get this place picked up." Mama would push her chair back from the table, leaving the cards for one of us kids to pick up. She had bigger fish (well, really hamburger) to fry. "Linney, go get me a pack of hamburger out of the freezer. David, you clean up the living room, and Kay, you take care of this."

"This" she defined with a sweep of her arm at the dining room table, where we'd been holed up for a full day of our summer vacation. "I've *got* to get dressed!"

At some point in the day, one of my brothers might have pulled on a pair of shorts and his cowboy boots. However, as the sun started dropping in the sky, we were usually still in our pajamas.

Hot summer mornings often began with my two younger brothers and me pulling out a game board or a pack of cards. We preferred canasta and gin rummy, but liked those games best when four people played. That meant we needed Mama. She'd listen to our pleas, pick up her cup of coffee, take it to the dining room table, and agree to a couple of hands, always adding, "And then I've got work to do." Of course, we didn't need to beg too hard, because Mama loved playing games and cards. We joked that she wanted three kids so she could always play a hand of cards. And, of course, one hand leads to another—and another.

Now, we didn't live in some kind of poker hangout, pool hall combination. No, a suburban ranch housed our family of five. Daddy worked in Oak Ridge, Tennessee, at one of the government plants, and Mama took care of us kids. Summer was our favorite season. We went strawberry-picking, planted a garden, loved water-skiing on the Clinch River, camped as much as possible, and spent Sunday mornings and Wednesday nights at Cedar Grove Baptist Church.

On those card-playing days, we didn't do a lick of work; we just stayed in our pajamas all day. We laughed and we strategized. We learned about each other: who could bluff, and who couldn't, who always wanted the high cards, and who would take a risk. Mama told stories of growing up in North Georgia with thirteen brothers and sisters, and we'd talk about the happenings in our lives. At some point we ate bologna sandwiches, but we never stopped playing. In my memory, the house stayed dark. We didn't even open the curtains, and that only added to the secret pleasure of the day.

Mama liked having kids. And she especially liked having us for her kids. She never played easy with us. We all tried our best to win, but we always laughed a lot while doing it. Mama knew us, and told us about ourselves as we laid down the cards and picked them up again. "There goes Kay grabbing up the aces. She likes those high cards. She wants to win fast."

Because she knew us so well, she boldly told the world who we were and didn't back down. "No, David doesn't have a learning problem. He just doesn't want to do the work. He's only seven, and he beats his older brother and sister, his daddy, and me at *Clue*." Then she told us how she looked at the school psychologist and asked, "Have you ever played *Clue*?" If she knew where to find that psychologist today, she'd be the first to wave David's college degree in computer programming in his face.

Then there was the complicity we shared after we'd played the last hand. Mama flung that frozen block of hamburger into a pot on the stove to defrost it. We threw open the curtains and dashed off to put on our clothes. Cleaning up was a part of the day. Mama played hooky with us, while her day's work waited. We giggled a lot during those thirty minutes of scurrying around. We weren't trying to keep it a secret from Daddy how we'd spent our day. Mama always told him as soon as he came in. No, the giddiness came because we'd stepped outside what the world said was good and right.

You just don't sit inside on a beautiful summer day with the curtains drawn, and you definitely can't still be in your pajamas at suppertime. Adults have too much to do, too many things on their mind, to sit around playing games. Besides, who wants to play with a bunch of kids? Where's the fun in playing with a seven-year-old when you're eleven?

Mama tossed off the confines of being an adult, and we rose above the passivity of *just being kids*. We stepped outside the world as we knew it for a day.

God watched our little family and surely smiled at the lessons Mama provided. Those times we left the regular routine taught me that the world doesn't always know what is good and right. What the neighbors might say isn't nearly as important as what your heart says. Mama knew that a day of just being, loving, and laughing—a day of ignoring what the world wants to force down our throats—is sometimes needed. Those card-playing days happened in the summers of the late '60s and early '70s. Now, as an adult, I know that the world outside my house was falling apart during those hot and humid days. Mama couldn't keep Watergate, or Vietnam, or death out of our world, but she did teach us to step out of that world occasionally.

I remember those days when I hear God calling me to stop, take some time, and spend a day with him. I want to tell him how busy I am, how much I need to get done. Then I recall a darkened house, bologna rings on the kitchen counter, three kids in pajamas laughing and loving their mama, still in her robe as she deals the cards.

You know, God, maybe I do have the time.

WAVING AT MISS VELMA

LANITA BRADLEY BOYD

When my father and mother went into the general store down the road from their house for a routine purchase of some staple items, the scene was familiar—middle-aged Velma, daughter of the store owner, was sitting with her mother picking up store gossip. On this day, however, Velma rose from her seat, verbally attacking my mother, yelling, "Who do you think you are, making my little Bobby Joe stand in the corner? Some teacher you are! Picking on my poor boy!"

Mother had had a hard day of teaching, her students spanning four grades, and at that moment had no memory of what had precipitated the punishment of Bobby Joe. She stood there while Velma progressed to obscenities that sent mothers with young ones scurrying from the store.

When Mother and Daddy got home—both having taken the abuse in silence—she said, "Lawrence, I'm never going into that store again."

"You don't really mean that," he responded. He knew her well. By morning she had resolved to turn the situation around.

"I think I need some cheese," she decided that afternoon on the way home from school.

She went back to the store, where Velma's father, John, waited on her. My mother, only twenty-one years old at the time, decided to address the incident directly. She said, "Mr. John, I didn't care for what happened here yesterday."

Mother thought that was the end of it. But when she got home from the store, Daddy came in, shaking his head.

"Here's our cream," he said. "It wasn't picked up."

In their rural community of 1944, Velma's husband was the local dairy driver who picked up the farmers' cream and took it to the dairy every morning. This time he had left theirs at the side of the road to sour.

After that, they had to take it to the dairy themselves, and soon they quit selling cream altogether, because the long trip every day was more trouble than it was worth. Instead, they simply gave the cream to neighbors.

Beginning that day, Mother started a determined campaign. Every time she saw Velma or her husband, Alfred, she would smile and say hello. If she were in the car, she would give a big wave. Frequently she would write positive notes about Bobbie Joe, and she showered him with love and concern.

Toward the end of the school year, Velma's husband, Alfred, flagged Mother down at the edge of his driveway, catching her in mid-wave. *Oh, no*, she thought. *What now?*

"Miss Mary," he said, the words tumbling out as though if he paused he might lose courage. "Miss Mary, down at the dairy we have this new kind of oleomargarine. It's colored yellow, and it's in sticks." He shoved a package at her. "I thought you might like to try some." And he was gone.

Two weeks later, he flagged her down again. This time he held a cardboard cylinder. Thrusting it at her, he said, "These here are canned biscuits. Ever hear of that? No, I didn't figger you did. Thought you might like to try them."

Mother had made a point that Miss Velma's husband, at least, had responded to. But this woman of courage and zeal did not stop there.

As the years passed, Mother and Daddy had three children of their own. We children knew nothing of the original conflict between Mother and Miss Velma. All we knew was that Mother would remind us to "wave at Miss Velma, children" every time we passed her house, whether or not we could see her. Mother suspected that Miss Velma was peering out from behind the curtains and would be pleased that we had waved at her.

Year after year when the church put together fruit baskets at Christmas, Mother volunteered to take a basket to Miss Velma and Mr. Alfred. Each year when the route for the carol singers was being planned, Mother would quietly add their names, even though they were neither elderly nor shut-ins.

I never understood what I perceived as my mother's fondness for this bitter, tight-lipped woman. Sometimes, as the oldest child, I'd be the one sent to Miss Velma's door with the message, "Here's some coconut cake Mother thought you'd enjoy," or "Mother thought maybe you could use these extra tomatoes, since we have a good crop this year." But most of the time it was Mother herself who went to the dreaded door, smiling all the way up the front walk.

Every summer our rural church would have a "gospel meeting" and Mother would always invite Miss Velma and Mr. Alfred to no avail. Finally, when I was a teenager, Mother came bouncing in from one of her many trips to Miss Velma's. "Miss Velma and Mr. Alfred are coming to church tonight!" she announced, eyes brimming with tears.

"Great!" we all responded, secretly fearing they would let Mother down.

Not only did they come that night but also the next night and the next. Emboldened, Mother said, "Miss Velma, what if Lawrence and I come over and study the Bible with you and Mr. Alfred?"

"I think that's a good idea," Miss Velma said, nodding slowly.

The studies touched their hearts, and they were baptized into Christ, remaining faithful Christians for the rest of their lives.

After I married and lived out of state, I rarely saw Miss Velma, though sheer habit brought a wave every time I occasionally passed her house. Sometimes Mother would mention that Miss Velma had given her a quilt top, or some preserves, or some purchased gift.

One day when I was at Mother's, Miss Velma, stooped and trembly now, stopped by for a visit. "You know, Lanita, your mama is the finest woman that ever lived," she said. "I've never had a friend like her—ever. I never had a sister, either, but if I'd had one, I'd have wanted her to be just like Mary. You're a lucky young woman to have a mother like her."

I agreed but didn't think much of her comments at the time. After she left, Mother decided to tell me the history of their friendship. "I do love her now," Mother said, "but there were many years when I didn't. I just kept thinking that I was a Christian and the only way she would ever change was to experience how a Christian is different from other people. I just didn't want Satan to win on this one." She smiled. "And it has paid off in multitudes of ways."

Walking in his steps, a Christian schoolteacher became Jesus to a sinful woman and helped her to live for God. Now as I encounter difficult people in a variety of situations, my natural tendency is to turn away and deal with them as little as possible. But remembering the example of my mother, I remind myself not to give up on the unlovable, but instead to "wave at Miss Velma."

A PURSE FULL OF
LOVE AND WONDER

ANITA HIGMAN

When I was just a girl, one of my favorite things to do was to look through my mother's purse while sitting in church on a Sunday morning. My mother allowed me to do this, most likely, to ensure the minister a service that would be squirm-free on my end of the pew. But as I reflect, I think these encounters did a bit more for me than that.

These purse-sifting, trinket-finding expeditions did indeed keep me from embarrassing my family. So I suppose my mom's ploy was clever and effective. (As a side note, it was surprising how much of the pastor's words I absorbed even as I took in the treasures buried in her handbag!)

Yes, that pocketbook was full of grown-up mysteries. My little fingers would shuffle around to discover a chunky bottle of cologne, which sparkled in the light and seemed to be a well of scent that never ran dry. I found and tasted bitter mints that were supposed to freshen one's breath, but perhaps did little more than threaten to upset one's breakfast. I gobbled up red oval drops that were meant for coughs, but tasted suspiciously like cherry candy. Although I can't recall, there must have been the usual creams and powders and mirrors that light up the curious eyes of little girls. But the other part I do remember well were the pastel tissues that my mother would show me how to magically make into carnation flowers with a hairpin and some folding and tearing finesse. Yes, that vinyl carryall was ripe with joys.

I loved it that my mother allowed me to see inside her life that way. There was an intimacy, a special connection with her, when I explored the feminine things she chose to have near her. She never seemed worried I would lose anything, make a mess of her purse, or see something too private. She never snatched the purse away from me in anger or gave me looks that said I was just a hopeless little snoop. It was a simple and gentle love offering to her little girl.

I felt bathed in love to be allowed to gaze into that well of enchantment.

Even now I have the same feeling when I swish my hand through a glistening stream, gaze at a blazing sunset, or peer into the delicate folds of an iris or a rose. Through those intimate encounters with my mother's most personal possession, her purse, she left subtle yet poignant spiritual impressions on me. Such a gesture not only helped me to see God's character of wonder and love but also to see the way in which God gives his gifts. He loves to shower good things on us, never snatching them back in anger. Instead, he looks on lovingly, graciously encouraging us, smiling down on us, and desiring to bestow on us and trust us with an open treasury brimming with love and wonder. For me, it is an insight into our Creator that I will never tire of thinking about!

———

Some years ago my mother died, and I am certain she is celebrating the awesome delights of heaven. Down here on earth, I am still cherishing those endearing memories that left lasting fingerprints on me—truths revealed through innocent play and a purse full of love and wonder.

CHRISTMAS

MARSHA DRAKE

from *The Proverbs 31 Lady and Other Impossible Dreams*

I was hobbling around the kitchen preparing a turkey to cook for Christmas Day. I peered out the kitchen window to look for the boys who had been playing football in a nearby vacant lot. "The wind is really whipping!" I exclaimed to myself.

At dinnertime, John seemed unusually quiet. "Anything wrong?" I asked.

"The weather has me a bit concerned, that's all. Nothing to worry about though," he said lightly and cuffed George playfully on the chin.

As we ate, I could hear the rain pelting on the rooftop and the wind howling around the house.

I was in the middle of serving dessert when I heard some unusual sounds from outside. Fear immediately gripped me. Trying to cover my panic, I casually inquired of John, "Do you hear that?"

"It's the river," he replied seriously. "The current is becoming so strong that it's disturbing the riverbed." He rose from the table and walked toward the telephone in the kitchen. "I'd better call a quick meeting to see what we're going to do about it."

I heard him talking in a low tone, and then he returned to the table. "What is it?" I asked in a worried voice.

He calmly gazed at his three sons and me. "Why don't you finish your dessert now," he smiled reassuringly at the boys. Then, "Martha, I'd like a quick word with you."

"Sure," I agreed as terror crawled up my spine. I followed him to our bedroom. "What is it, John?" Dread pushed all other emotion out of my consciousness.

"Flood," John said quietly.

"Here?" I couldn't believe my ears. Floods happened to other people, not to us.

"Now, listen carefully," he continued. "You may have to evacuate—"

"Me? Us? Where will you be?" Apprehension at having to face a crisis without John caused my knees to turn to water. "Don't worry, Martha." He was already grabbing his car keys from the dresser. "You can do it."

"Where will you *be*?" I repeated while numbness spread through me.

"Martha!" John squeezed my shoulders hard. "Get a hold of yourself. Where is your faith?" He relaxed his grip and continued in a reproving voice, "Somebody has to go, and I don't need to have you to worry about too. You'll be fine."

His last phrase echoed in my brain as he spoke quietly to each of the boys. A horn honked outside in the blackness, and he was gone. *You'll be fine*—hadn't I heard that somewhere? Then I remembered. Viv had told me I would be fine when I began sewing my blouse. "My blouse wasn't fine. My blouse was horrible," I whispered to myself.

Mechanically I did as John had instructed. We finished dessert, and I tried to appear unafraid as the boys and I cleaned up the table and washed the dishes. "We won't use the dishwasher," I advised. I didn't have any reason, except that doing dishes would keep us all busy.

"Listen, guys!" shouted Joe in excitement. He ran to the living room window and opened it wide. A torrent of rain blew in, and the noise of the river sounded like the [Stawamus] Chief [Mountain] beginning to crumble.

"Close that window!" I commanded.

Six eyes bored into mine and read my alarm. Joe closed the window without argument.

"Now listen, kids," I began, "I don't want to worry you, but Dad says there may be a flood—"

"A flood? Hooray!" whooped George. "Just like on television!" He began to race around the room.

"Hampst!" shrieked Joe. "Where is Hampst?" Terror filled his eyes as he began a frantic search around the room.

John Jr. stared at me, his blue eyes clear, and asked, "Did Dad say anything about Specimen?"

"Maybe you should call her in," I replied, feeling faint. "Excuse me for a minute, will you?" I fled to our bedroom, closed the door, and fell on my knees.

"Help me, God," I prayed, "I'm so afraid."

Right in the middle of the storm, I reached for my Bible. And while terror shook my body, alone with God, I read His Word and was comforted. "Bid the older women . . . to give good counsel. . . . They will wisely train the young women to be . . . self-controlled . . . subordinating themselves to their husbands, that the word of God may not be exposed to reproach—blasphemed or discredited" (Titus 2:3–5 AMP).

"You'll be fine," I could almost hear John's voice. I rose from my knees and headed for the living room.

"Have you found Hampst yet?" My calm voice sounded foreign to my ears. George sensed a difference too. I could tell from his answer.

"Joe isn't here, Mom. He went to his room." He came over and wrapped his arms around my waist. "You look brave too. Just like Daddy."

"Good," I said, giving him a bear hug. "Now, how about getting Ben ready to travel?"

"We goin' somewhere? Great!" His eyes flashed with excitement. "I'll get lots of carrots for Ben! Enough for a whole week!" He ran to the kitchen, and I heard the fridge door opening and carrots being dumped on the floor. For once I didn't care about the amount.

"Oh, for the faith of a child," I said softly as I headed for Joe's room. I had a feeling he would be there, trying to hide his fear about Hampst the Second being lost.

Opening the door a crack, I called, "Joe?"

"Come on in, Mom," came a discouraged voice.

He sat on the edge of his bed with his head in his hands. "Did you find Hampst?" I asked gently, sure that he hadn't.

"Oh, Mom!" Tears of anguish coursed down his cheeks, and my heart suffered with him for his loss. I hugged him tightly and felt his misery.

Smoothing his hair with my hand, I suggested, "You know, Joe, God loves Hampst too. Did you ever think about asking Him to help us find Hampst?"

Joe looked up at me, hope lighting his brown eyes. "Could we?" He wiped his tears with his shirtsleeves.

Together we prayed about Hampst the Second. Then I said, "Now you go and look for him, and we'll leave the results to God."

"Okay, Mom," he replied, and he was off like a shot, calling "Hampst! Here boy! Hampst!"

John Jr. returned from the basement. He was soaking wet and covered with mud. "I found Specimen," he announced proudly. "I've got her tied up in the basement."

"Excellent!" I commended him for his responsible behavior. "Now, how about you changing into some dry clothes?"

"Okay!" he exclaimed, beaming. "Anything else?"

"Yes, there is something more for you to do. Dad said we may have to evacuate—"

"You mean leave the house?" his eyes widened in surprise.

"Yes." I continued calmly, "I need you to collect our sleeping bags, a couple of Bibles, and whatever else you think we might need for an overnight stay." I paused to take a deep breath. "Do you think you can handle it?" I patted him on the shoulder. He seemed inches taller than he had an hour earlier.

"You bet!" he replied, racing off on his mission.

"So far, so good. Thanks, Lord," I whispered. I stood in the hall for a moment, wondering what to do next. A strange urge to walk into the living room hit me, and without thinking, I strolled slowly into the room. Something scurried along the edge of the couch—one tiny, brown ball of fluff propelled by four pink feet. "Hampst!" I exclaimed softly. "Joe! Come quickly!"

In a second Joe stood at the other end of the couch. "Hampst!"

Five minutes later, Hampst the Second sat munching sunflower seeds, safe in his cage. "Thanks again, God!" I said softly as I began to prepare some sandwiches and a thermos of hot chocolate.

One by one the boys popped into the kitchen. "Hampst is ready to travel," announced Joe happily.

"Specimen is waiting. And I got a bag of dog food for her," said John Jr.

"Ben has enough carrots for about a month!" George flitted from the step stool to the stove in eager anticipation.

"Good," I replied, finishing the sandwiches. "Now, how would you like to get me the picnic hamper?"

Three boys shot down the stairs and reappeared in minutes bearing the insulated case, three bags of marshmallows and some potato chips. The disaster had taken on the air of a picnic outing as they scurried to gather some candles and matches.

What a Christmas Eve, I thought as I tidied the kitchen and packed the rest of the food in the hamper. "Better turn off the lights on the Christmas tree and unplug the television," I ordered.

We had just finished our preparations when the noise of the boulders bumping in the rushing river could no longer be ignored. Alarmed, I spoke quietly to the boys, "I think I'll just take a quick look out front. I'll be right back." Descending the stairs to the front door, I looked outside. Our maple tree bent in the wind almost to the ground, and leaves and sticks whirled everywhere. "I wonder if we're supposed to leave?" I asked myself. Suddenly I felt we should go. Quickly climbing the stairs, I called, "Boys, turn off the lights in your rooms. I think we'll leave now."

I was surprised at how well the boys handled themselves as we loaded the car, the dog, the guinea pig, and Hampst the Second.

Just as I was backing the car out of the driveway, the river jumped its banks. A wall of water hurtled down the street toward us. As I floored the accelerator, the water was already sweeping away lawns and driveways.

"Just like the Indianapolis 500!" yelled George as I squealed the tires and the car lurched forward.

It was the wildest ride of my life. We hit the bottom of the hill just before the water in a tiny rivulet exploded over the sides of the road and buried it in mud. And we reached the top of the hill just before lightning dropped a telephone pole across the intersection leading into town.

Police officers met us at every point. They were carrying radio receivers, and we could hear the crackle of voices on the short-waves as they waved us on toward the elementary school in the center of town. "How brave they are!" I exclaimed. They stood without protection in the middle of the storm, directing others toward safety.

At two o'clock on Christmas morning, most of the residents were in safe areas. I still hadn't seen John, but I heard that he was out along the riverbanks with other men, checking the rising water level. I prayed that God would keep him and the others safe.

At 3:00 A.M., the boys finally slept on the gymnasium floor beside me. All around us were others who had been forced to leave their homes to the mercy of the flood.

Unknown to me, John and some other men had gone to check the old dam high above the town. If that gave way, tons of water would cover the whole valley as it had early in the century, with terrible loss of life.

Sitting on the school gym floor, I prayed for the safety of our town. I knew nothing about the disaster which threatened, but I did know that Christmas Day two thousand years ago, God poured out His love on mankind. I asked Him to save us all this Christmas Day. Tears glistened, then dripped to the floor. I sat with my head on my knees interceding for friends and strangers. I left the results with God.

At 5:00 A.M. I was in the arms of my husband. He had returned to find us huddled in the school gymnasium. "Oh, John! I'm so thankful you're safe," I whispered as I hugged him.

He said nothing, but the expression of his face told me more than a thousand words. He was tired, but pleased that the threat was over. "The water has begun to recede," he said simply.

"How long will we have to stay here?" I asked him.

Putting his arm around my shoulder, he answered, "There may be another storm on the way."

"We will be fine," I said with conviction.

John remembered his earlier remark and his rebuke. His eyes softened. Looking deep into my eyes, he whispered, "Merry Christmas, Excellent Wife."

From him it was a compliment of the highest order. I recalled another verse I'd read while kneeling in terror in our bedroom: "Guide the household, [and] not give opponents of the faith occasion for slander or reproach" 1 Timothy 5:14 (AMP).

A wave of love for my husband swept over me, followed by overwhelming gratitude to God for the tiny baby Jesus, who had graced a manger and changed the course of mankind. Squeezing John's hands tightly, I replied simply, "Thank you."

SECTION *Four*

The GRACE OF A MOTHER

THE LEMONADE STAND

CHONDA PIERCE

from *Second Row, Piano Side*

O ur favorite thing to do on Easter Sunday was to see what the rich kids were wearing—'cause we knew that's what we'd be wearing the next Easter.

Along with scripture verses, choruses, manners, and the proper dress code, the greatest thing my mother passed on to us was the gift of adaptation. I am almost certain that my mother invented the phrase "When life gives you lemons . . ." Mom and Dad instilled in us not only the joy of a good glass of lemonade but also the thrill of making it yourself!

We never considered ourselves well off financially. We seldom considered ourselves poor. We simply didn't consider *ourselves*. My wardrobe was filled with hand-me-downs and homemade dresses my grandmother would send us every fall for the upcoming school year. When we wore shoes, they were usually tennis shoes or sandals. Since we lived in the South, barefoot was vogue!

There did come a brief time when the realization that "We *are* poor" hit us all. Mother couldn't find a job. Dad had just accepted a call to a small church in Orangeburg, South Carolina. Mike had gone to a college 500 miles away, and Charlotta was soon to follow. I can remember hearing Mom and Dad argue about the possibility of getting food stamps. I don't think it was as much a matter of pride as it was that Mom still didn't consider us desperate enough. She would say, "But what if someone else needs them more?"

As I sat at the dinner table eating for the fifth time that week a sandwich made with government cheese and grilled with government butter, I looked at her and said, "Mom, who could need 'em worse than us?"

So one afternoon Mom and I stood in the food stamp line for more than three hours. Of course, after we got them, the whole family wanted in on the selection process at the grocery store. Grocery shopping had never been so exciting. Everyone was thrilled to pick out the food, but as soon as we approached the checkout counter, they all scrambled to the car—except for Mom and me. When Mother handed the girl at the Piggly Wiggly our little booklet, I grinned at Mother and said in my most Southern belle, Scarlett O'Hara voice, "I'll tell the driver to bring the limo around, Mother, and pick us up at the door. I know how you hate to wait in this summer heat." When the food stamps ran out, we went back to grilled cheese until things began to pick up at the church again.

Mother had toyed a long time with the idea of going to nursing school. When she heard that Baptist Hospital in Columbia, South Carolina, was offering a two-year Licensed Practical Nurse (LPN) course, she decided that this would be the year. She and Dad argued about her decision for hours—but for some reason, Mother truly felt nursing school was something she was called to do. She borrowed the money from her mother, and at the age of 40 off to school she went.

She drove 91 miles round trip to nursing school every day. Cheralyn and I made flash cards and quizzed her for exams. She amazed us all. Mother had not been in school in 22 years and would have failed chemistry in high school twice had it not been for the tutor her mom and dad had hired during her senior year. She passed nursing school with flying colors, and we proudly attended her graduation from LPN school. (Dad had refused to attend—but near the end of the ceremony we noticed him on the back row of that huge auditorium in Columbia.)

While Mom was in nursing school, Cheralyn and I had almost full responsibility of the house. We had our regular chores to do as well as cooking most of the meals. We were proud of our diverse menus: macaroni and cheese, peanut butter and jelly, Froot Loops—and on special occasions (or Friday, whichever came first) *hot dogs!*

Did I mention that we lived on a tight budget? We had a few poundings from the church folks—but you get mostly dusty, dented cans of yams and cranberry sauce at those things! So Cheralyn and I decided the answer to our menu problem was simply to grow our own garden. We worked for hours getting the soil ready. We saved our money and went down to the local hardware store and purchased seed packets of green beans, corn, cucumbers, and tomatoes. The weeds outgrew our patience, and our sandy Southern soil could produce nothing—nothing but cucumbers, that is.

They were everywhere! We had a long vine of cucumbers that stretched from the front porch of our house, across the church parking lot, and up the steps of the fellowship hall. We made cucumber sandwiches, cucumber salad, fried cucumbers—anything you could make with cucumbers, we made. Some things you couldn't make with cucumbers we made anyway. And we ate them all.

Then just like the plagues finally ended in Egypt, we received a sweet reprieve from our cucumber suppers. A man in our church raised hogs for his chain of barbecue restaurants. He called the house one evening to say that the next morning he would be stopping by with a package for the pastor and his family. Hallelujah!

Cheralyn and I rewrote our menu for the next month: barbecued pork chops, ribs, ham, bacon—we even made plans for the ears and the feet. We set the table that night for tomorrow's dinner. We were so excited we could hardly sleep. (Or maybe it was the cucumbers!)

Nevertheless, as promised, an old pickup truck pulled into the driveway the next afternoon. A kind old farmer climbed out of his truck carrying a huge package wrapped in brown paper. The front of his apron was bloody, but we hardly pitied the beast we would dine on for the next few weeks. We could smell something spicy and delicious as he set the package on the counter. We had envisioned a huge country ham, perhaps a pork roast, maybe slabs of bacon. We couldn't wait for him to leave so we could dive in.

Mother thanked him very kindly, and as the front door clicked shut, Cheralyn and I ripped open our mouth-watering feast. There it was—a fresh, meaty, 15-pound roll of bologna! Now don't get me wrong. I don't dislike bologna. But a couple of skinny little preacher's kids had waited all day long for pork chops and had gotten bologna—disappointing bologna.

When mother fixed supper that night, we were surprised to see something shaped like pork chops on our plates. Mother had used some of her arts and crafts skills to cut little pork chop shapes out of the bologna and fried it until it was crisp. Served with cold, sliced cucumbers and cornbread, Mom showed us how to make lemonade out of lemons.

The next day the doorbell rang. A young lady stood on our porch and explained to Mother how she had noticed the church next door and wondered if we knew how to reach the pastor. Mother invited her in. With watery eyes, she told Mother that her children were hungry and that her husband had been out of work for several months. Her food stamps had run out too. Without question, Mom quickly filled a grocery sack with cucumbers and cut our much-needed roll of bologna in half and shared it with this stranger. They shared a glass of lemonade before she left, and we never saw her again.

Be kind and compassionate to one another, forgiving each other, just as in Christ God forgave you. (Ephesians 4:32)

PERFECTLY ADAPTED

ELISABETH ELLIOT

from *A Path Through Suffering*

There is nothing arbitrary in the different shapes of the seed-vessels. . . . The fine sand-like grain of this snapdragon needs storing in a capsule—such a quaint one it is (whether most like a bird or a mouse sitting on a twig is hard to say)—but it is a perfectly adapted treasure-bag for the delicate things.

My friend Judy Squier of Portola Valley, California, is one of the most cheerful and radiant women I know. I met her first in a prayer meeting at the beginning of a conference. She was sitting in a wheelchair and I noticed something funny about her legs. Later that day I saw her with no legs at all. In the evening she was walking around with a cane. Of course I had to ask her some questions. She was gracious, humorous, and forthright in her answer. Born with no legs, she has prostheses which she uses sometimes but they are tiresome, she said (laughing), and she often leaves them behind.

When I heard of a little boy named Brandon Scott, born without arms or legs, I asked Judy if she would write to his parents. She did. She told them that this was at least a hundred times harder for them than it would be for Brandon, for "a birth defect by God's grace does not rob childhood of its wonder, nor is a child burdened by high expectations."

Judy described her life not as less-than-average; or even average or ordinary, but as extraordinary, because she is convinced that a loving Heavenly Father oversees the creative miracles in the inner sanctum of each mother's womb (Ps. 139), and that in His sovereignty there are no accidents.

We may look at the various ways in which each of us is called to suffer as the Master Designer's shaping of the vessels meant to bear the seed of the divine life. The design of each is directly related to the function, and thus He gives to each something unique to offer, something no other is capable of rendering back to Him.

The One who formed the perfect seed-vessels according to the shape of the seed they carry formed Judy, and Judy has a special message to bear, a testimony which deals a heavy blow to the "quality of life" arguments for abortion. She goes on:

"What we judge to be 'tragic—the most dreaded thing that could happen,' I expect we'll one day see as the awesome reason for the beauty and uniqueness of our life and our family. I expect that's why James 1:2 is a favorite verse of mine. Phillips' translation puts it this way: 'When all kinds of trials and temptations crowd into your lives, my brothers, don't resent them as intruders, but welcome them as friends! Realize that they come to test your faith and to produce in you the quality of endurance.' "

Judy is the mother of three beautiful little girls who she said were "popping in and out" so that she couldn't think too deeply as she was writing her letter, "but I give you a moment of down-to-earth real life which I am good at, since I am a very 'earthy' person.

"Being Christian didn't shield my family from the pain and tears that came with my birth defect. In fact, ten years ago when David and I interviewed our parents for a Keepsake Tape, I was stunned to hear my mother's true feelings. I asked her to tell the hardest thing in her life. Her response: 'The day Judy Ann was born and it still is. . . .' And yet when we as a family look back over the years, our reflections are invariably silenced by the *wonder* of God's handiwork.

"Getting married and becoming a mother were dreams I never dared to dream, but God, the doer of all miracles, intended that my life be blessed with an incredible husband and three daughters."

In closing, she tells the Scott family that they have been "chosen in a special way to display His unique Masterwork. I pray that your roots will grow deep down into the faithfulness of God's loving plan, that you will exchange your inadequacy for the adequacy of Jesus' resurrection power, and that you will be awed as you witness the fruits of the Spirit manifested in your family. 'What the caterpillar calls the end of the world, the Creator calls a butterfly.' "

A PRICELESS GIFT

MEGHAN J. ROSSI

I grasped the receiver with a white-knuckled grip and listened as the phone on the other end began to ring—once, twice, three, then four times. *Maybe she's working late at school. I'll hang up and try again later.*
"Hello?" *Too late.*

"Mom?"

"Hi! What's wrong?" *How does she know something is wrong? Very wrong.*

"Mom, I—" I dissolved into tears. I should have thought through what I was going to say before I dialed her number. Or maybe I should have sent her a card. Then again, Hallmark has yet to create the perfect card to help young unmarried women tell their mothers they are pregnant. Besides, I'd just turned nineteen, I had two and a half years of college still ahead of me, my boyfriend's parents were making no effort to conceal the fact that they didn't like me and they continually sought ways to get me out of his life—*I* was the one who needed a card.

"Are you okay?" Mom tried again to get me to open up to her. I sobbed some more into the phone.

"Are you pregnant?"

"Yes."

"Is Shawn the father?"

"Yes."

After seconds of silence ticked away, she said, "Come home. We'll work this out. It's going to be okay. Just come home this weekend and we'll talk things through. You're going to be okay."

I don't know what my mom did when she hung up the phone that afternoon; I'm guessing she cried a lot. Thanks to her calm support, however, I felt a twinge of hope that everything would be okay. It was the first hint of optimism I'd felt since my doctor's appointment.

A year and a half before all of this happened, my mom gave me her blessing and financial support to attend a state college hundreds of miles away from home with thousands of other students. With high hopes for my future, Mom sent me to college and trusted me to make good choices in spite of her absence from my daily routine. However, it wasn't long before I broke that trust by experimenting with alcohol.

My new friends and roommates asked me to go to parties at fraternities, upperclassmen's apartments, and campus bars. I'd never been invited to drinking parties before, so I took my first drink to fit in and satisfy my curiosity; I kept drinking, because then I didn't feel so awkward and nervous while standing in a room full of strangers. My solution worked too well.

While the beer chased away my inhibitions—especially with men—it also left me with little or no common sense. Too many mornings I was left with either embarrassing memories or no recollection of what I'd done or with whom. For three semesters I pursued my party lifestyle at school and then slipped back into my good-girl persona before going home for weekend visits. The truth caught up with me eventually; I'm just glad it happened while I was dating Shawn.

We'd been friends for half our lives but we didn't start dating until we were college sophomores. Naturally, Shawn was terrified by my pregnancy; but he took responsibility for his part, never considered abortion as an option, and he stayed by my side while his parents pressured him to stop seeing me.

I knew my mom wasn't ready to face Shawn yet, so I drove home alone that weekend. I didn't know what to expect when I pulled into the driveway. Mom had been positive and encouraging on the phone, but how would she act now that she'd had a few days to wrestle with the reality of my situation? What would she say when she saw me?

As it turned out, she didn't say much. She hugged me, cried with me, and continued to reassure me that things would be okay. She also didn't make me feel worse by trying to punish me or by telling me how many people I'd hurt by getting pregnant. Instead, during the coming months she let me lean on her in a number of meaningful ways.

To escape the focus of small-town gossips and to shield my family from as much shame as possible, I lived on campus that summer and took two classes.

It was encouraging to know that my mom was only a phone call away. We spoke to each other often. She'd always been a good listener, but now I learned to appreciate the way she would let me talk as I tried to sort things out for myself. She never tried to tell me how I should think or feel.

Once I called and asked her to go to the clinic with me when I had to undergo a three-hour test for gestational diabetes. She didn't hesitate before agreeing to come, even though it meant driving two and a half hours each way. When I began to feel lightheaded during the last of the three blood tests, it was so comforting to have my mother with me.

During that summer apart, she wrote me letters to remind me that I wasn't alone and sent me an occasional care package containing items like food, a daily calendar full of inspirational thoughts and Scripture verses, and treats like a Snickers bar or a stuffed animal to make me smile. Most important, Mom never made me feel like I was a bad person, never threatened to kick me out of the house or family, never scolded me or treated me like a five-year-old child.

When Shawn and I met with an adoptive couple's lawyer, Mom came along and made sure we asked the right questions. This appointment happened to be the first time my mom saw Shawn since learning about my pregnancy, yet she treated him with kindness and respect, no matter how she might have felt toward him at the time.

I don't know what I would have done without my mom's support during that difficult period in my life. She loved me, forgave me for the hurt and pain I caused my family, and never stopped encouraging me. Before I discovered I was pregnant, I'd taken her faith in me for granted and thoughtlessly crushed it during my first three semesters of wild campus living. Yet she stayed by my side. She prayed for me, my boyfriend (who is now her son-in-law), and also for the baby—her first grandson. She came to the hospital when it was time for me to deliver, even though it meant driving almost three hours in the middle of the night.

In spite of the fact that I'd obviously made some terrible choices before getting pregnant, Mom didn't interfere with the decisions Shawn and I made during the pregnancy and throughout the adoption process. Mom never withdrew her love from me. I never sensed that she was ashamed of me. Instead, she repeatedly told me she was proud of me for choosing not to have an abortion, for making tough decisions, for going to my doctor's appointments, for staying on campus that summer in order to keep up in school, and for managing it all in spite of the great amount of shame and guilt I felt. Her pride in me never waned; it actually grew. Although I didn't give God much credit at the time, looking back it's obvious he provided everything I needed to survive the months of my pregnancy—my mom being the most important provision.

Shortly after my son was adopted, I realized that my life was never going to return to the normalcy I'd known the year before. I also discovered that while my partying lifestyle could never fill the void in my life, it was quickly making the void larger and deeper. I was searching for something more and found it about six weeks after we'd signed the adoption papers. While attending a Bible study with my brother, I listened as the others talked about God's Word like it made sense to them, shared about struggles in their lives with confidence in God's hope and peace, and sang joyful worship songs about what it meant to follow Jesus.

Meanwhile, I felt lousy. I was tired of pretending that my pregnancy hadn't affected me beyond the physical changes my body had gone through. I wanted to experience what they'd found, especially God's forgiveness and love. During the prayer time at the end of the study, my spirit of pride and defensiveness finally broke as I asked Jesus to come into my life and give me a fresh start.

I don't like to think about what could have happened if Mom had hung up on me when I made that difficult phone call, but I'm sure my life would be very different now if she had turned her back on me. I know I survived because of my mom's prayers, unwavering love, and the many ways she supported me tangibly with phone calls and letters and trips to visit me. But most of all I appreciate her willingness to give me a second chance. If she hadn't shown me such grace, I doubt I would have chosen to believe that God could do the same. The grace I received from my mom—and from God—taught me how important it is to extend grace to others when they've hurt or disappointed me. It truly is the greatest gift we can give to another person, and it's a priceless gift to receive.

NUMBER ONE FAN

DONNA LINVILLE

as told to B.J. Connor

After Mom dropped me off for my first day of high school, I watched her drive away. I was terrified. I had to brace myself to enter the building. School to me was a private hell, where the other kids considered me stupid—after all, I got D's and F's, and I had repeated seventh grade. They also made fun of my weight. I smoothed out the drop-waist navy blue sailor dress Mom had had a seamstress make for me, hoping the style would have a slimming effect on my 5-foot–6, 220-pound frame.

Mother had been praying for me since May and promised me this year would be different. All summer I wondered how. Would I miraculously shrink from a size 22 to a 10? That hadn't happened. Would kids finally accept me and stop calling me names like "Fatso"?

As I walked down the hall, a boy I knew from last year yelled, "Hey, Big Mama! You're back again!" My blue eyes welled with tears. Nothing had changed.

My life had turned upside-down when I was ten and Dad's job took us from Indianapolis to Tupelo, Mississippi, in the middle of the school year. Feeling inferior and backward socially and academically, I became shy and reclusive.

One teacher seemed to get sadistic pleasure from belittling me. He would start by asking, "Donna, what's the answer?"

I knew the answer, but I had such low self-esteem, I stammered, "I-I . . ."

In an exasperated tone, the teacher would say, "What's the answer, class? Give Donna the answer." It was a vicious cycle. I ballooned on the outside and closed up on the inside.

My parents took my self-esteem and poor academics very seriously. They worked extra hours to pay for me to go to summer school and have tutors and for a friend to sew me younger-looking styles than the matronly "plus sizes" on department store racks.

Every day I begged, "Mom, don't make me go to school—please!" I pretended to be sick. Once I put a thermometer in hot water and showed my Mom how high the mercury had zoomed. As supportive as my mother (who was a nurse) was, she wasn't fooled by the 106-degree temperature!

My junior high school principal thought I was mentally retarded and had gone as far as I could scholastically. He'd recommended I be physically and psychologically tested and placed in a special-education class. When he told this to my parents and me, we were stunned. Riding home, watching my parents from the backseat, I saw tears silently slide down my mother's cheeks. Just then she turned her head and exclaimed, "Sweetheart, you're brilliant! You've got it in you, Baby! It'll come out!"

My pediatrician and the psychiatrist who tested me had been kind. When I got through the tests, the psychiatrist said, "You did tremendously, Donna. You're not dumb; in fact, you're a very smart young lady. Something has happened to you that has locked you up inside."

Then he said to my parents, "Mr. and Mrs. Shepard, there is a butterfly inside Donna that wants to come out."

That summer Mom came home from her nursing supervisor job each evening and cooked supper for us, but sometimes she didn't eat herself. She was fasting and praying for me instead. One night, I overheard her in the living room: "Jesus, I don't know what's got my child closed up so that she cannot be all that you want her to be. But, God, break it!"

To me she said, "Next year you're going to high school, and you're going to be different. In September, Donna, you're going to be a jewel! I can't wait! God is going to change you!"

At the end of that first day of high school, I was so hurt and miserable that I hid in the girls' rest room, where I could cry in private.

My dream was to sing like the pastor's wife or a missionary I'd heard at church. I would love to sing like that! But then I thought, *Nah, I'm not good enough to do that, and I can't think right—I'm stupid.*

Our house was filled with music, from Dad's Rodgers and Hammerstein records to opera to "The Wizard of Oz." I came home from church singing hymns, although I was much too shy to consider joining the choir. While other kids my age were into the Beatles and Tupelo-born Elvis, my favorite voices were those of Julie Andrews and various gospel singers. At home, I sang in my bedroom, standing in front of my mirror, holding a hairbrush for a microphone.

Assuming I was alone in the school rest room, I started singing, holding a sustained high note like an opera singer. The acoustics were fantastic!

Suddenly I heard a cough in one of the stalls. I grabbed my books and hurried down the corridor. A female voice that sounded like a drill sergeant demanded, "Wait a minute! Come here! What's your name?"

I reluctantly turned around and saw a slender, attractive woman. I lowered my eyes and mumbled, "Uh, er, my name's Donna Shepard."

"Look at me!" she commanded. "Lift your head up! What's your name again?"

"Donna Shepard," I repeated nervously, wondering what kind of trouble I was in.

"Come to my office in the morning!" she ordered.

"Wha-what do you want me to do?"

"I want you to try out for chorale."

"I can't—I can't sing," I stammered.

"I don't ever want to hear you say again that you can't do something. Do you hear me?" she barked.

"Okay," I said meekly. "Wha—what's your name?" She told me she was Mrs. Stevens.

I ran out to the car, and Mom asked, "How was it?"

"Everybody's the same, but Mother!" I said haltingly, in wonderment, "There's a woman who wants me to try out in the morning for chorale!"

"Oh, Donna, do! I want you to do it!"

"Mother, I can't! I'm not going to! I can't! I can't!" I said breathlessly.

But the next morning I forced my feet toward the music room and inched toward the piano, trembling.

"Sing! Sing a song!" Mrs. Stevens said brusquely.

"All I know is a Jesus song."

"Sing a Jesus song then!"

"Amazing grace . . ." I began in a wobbly voice.

"Higher, higher! Look at me! Breathe!"

"Amazing grace . . ."

"Higher!"

"Amazing grace . . ."

"Higher!"

"Amazing grace . . ."

"Higher!"

When I thought my voice would surely lift the roof, she said, "Good! I want you to sing first soprano in my chorale."

"I can't . . ." I began.

"Enough! I never want to hear 'I can't' again from you."

I went home shaking. "Mother! Mother, I can't believe this! I'm in chorale, and I'm first soprano!"

"Oh, Donna, that's great!"

As I got involved in chorale, I became more confident, spoke up in class, and studied harder.

Six weeks later it was report card day—traditionally, a death march for me. But this time I went home and said, "Here, Mother, I got my report card." My family gathered around.

Mom took one look and exclaimed, "Oh, Shep! [my Dad's nickname] Oh, Lord! Oh, Baby!"

I had made honor roll.

I sang a duet at church and solos at school and church. My best song was "He Touched Me." A drama teacher insisted I join the debate team, and I wrote articles for the school newspaper. Mrs. Stevens encouraged me to try out for school musicals. One of my favorite parts was being the mother in "Bye Bye Birdie." My music teacher and my drama teacher changed my whole world.

When I sang and acted, I began to enjoy students who had seemed distant—like the cheerleaders. I was invited to parties. A girl I'd mistakenly thought was snobbish said, "Donna, you were just like a shadow to us; we didn't even know you existed."

Singing in the girls' sextet at school, I was cracking jokes when one girl said, "Donna, I would have never dreamed you were like you are."

"I didn't know who I was, either!" I said, surprised. God had changed me—not physically so much as by boosting my confidence, so that my intelligence and humor could blossom. Mom started a positive chain reaction when she prayed for me. My greatest fan reached the One who loves me even more than she does. Mother believes God has a plan for each person—and that included me.

Not only did I graduate from high school but I graduated with honors. And when students voted for the Friendliest Person in School, I was chosen number three out of 1,300!

I met my husband, Gary, in Bible college, and today I live my dream of being a pastor's wife who sings. I recently flew to almost forty places in one year to speak and sing about the Lord's goodness, and I was in charge of the program for twenty-five thousand at a church conference, where I spoke and sang a solo. I've sung in places as far away as Hong Kong and Papua New Guinea. Knowing God's love, I like to sing "You're Special to Jesus" to encourage others. I trace it all back to Mom's praying and God's answering with a music teacher with the voice of a drill sergeant.

When I sing, Mom's the first one to start clapping. She's the first to give a standing ovation. I say, "Mother, wait till someone else stands! Everybody knows you're my mother!"

And she says, "If you don't be quiet, I'm gonna get pom-poms!"

TUCKED IN

RACHEL WALLACE-OBERLE

Some of life's most precious moments have occurred when I'm going through the rituals of bedtime with my children. I'm sure, according to today's pell-mell-push-and-shove-to-grow-up world, they're beyond the age where such indulgences are necessary, but they still eagerly look forward to this evening ritual.

Thomas likes to hop up onto the arm of the sofa at the bottom of the stairs and await his piggyback ride. It won't be long before he'll be as tall as I am, and we'll have to forgo the piggybacks, but for now this routine is well established and cannot vary. I stand in front of him, he wraps his arms around my neck, hangs on, and up we go. On the way, we scuffle over turning on the light switch, lurch against the banister, bang into the bookcase, stagger into his room, and fall down on the bed. All of this is done with shrieks of protest and glee.

There are nights when the last thing I feel like doing is piggybacking a gangly ten-year-old boy up two flights of stairs. Yet lately I've been thinking these days are numbered; it won't be long before the requests for such delightful nonsense will dwindle and cease altogether.

Once I have managed to extricate myself from Thomas's never-ending stranglehold hugs, I cross the hall to Barrett's room. Barrett just celebrated his fourteenth birthday and prides himself on being independent, but his desire to be coddled surfaces periodically. He bounds up the stairs and calls out, "Tuck me in!" with such breezy confidence that my heart is touched; it simply doesn't occur to him that his wish might not be granted.

Everything has to be just so; his water light that changes colors and emits a steady buzzing stream of bubbles must be turned on. The blinds must be closed, the alarm clock set, the quilt folded and at the ready for a sudden drop in temperature, and the weather journal consulted and returned to its sacred spot on the night table. This is where I have made the most amazing discoveries; cocooned in blankets, far away from the cares of the day, all sorts of thoughts, feelings, hopes, and confessions tumble out of my teenage son.

Sometimes it's not until the tucking-in ritual that I am given crucial information that would have been greatly appreciated much sooner. In this dim and cozy sanctum of ancient stuffed animals, partially finished models, guitar equipment, and heaps of motorcycle magazines, I've been told why the French teacher lost her temper, what my nail clippers have been used to clip, and who climbed out the window when the teacher left the room to make photocopies.

I've learned that Thomas isn't always fast asleep in his bed as I have assumed, but happily camping out on the floor in his brother's room until the wee hours of the morning. It is here that an experiment was revealed involving vinegar, C.L.R., and the coffeemaker, which explains the foul-tasting pot of coffee I made several weeks ago. And this is also where I've been privileged to receive updates from Barrett's small-but-budding romance department.

By moonlight, we've discussed how to live with integrity, sibling rivalry, school bullies, God, unrequited love, career possibilities, books, movies, fears, expectations, and favorite restaurants. Often I've descended the stairs teary-eyed at the glimpse I've had of the sweetness of my boys' spirits.

When my sons are grown and gone, I wonder if the urge to tuck them in will be any less. Somehow I don't think so. I expect I'll fiercely cherish the tender moments in those darkened bedrooms and regret all the times I said I was too tired and shooed them off.

Someday Barrett and Thomas may be tucking in little ones of their own, but I pray no matter where they are as night falls, they will always feel my heart tiptoeing into the room, kissing them on the cheek, smoothing the quilt, and pulling the blinds.

BE AT THE GATE

ELLIE LOFARO

Rainy days and Mondays don't always get me down, but they sure make me sleepy—especially when the rainy day is a gloomy, chilly Monday in late fall. I encountered one of those last week. The laundry was folded and put away. The kitchen floor was mopped after heavy weekend traffic. The guest bedroom sheets were changed. The Bible study that I teach was prepared, and the Bible study that I attend was completed. So at 3:45, I plopped on the couch with a *Time* magazine. I knew the house would come alive with dramatic stories, snacks, homework, permission slips, and the like at precisely 4:02, as it does every weekday.

Lord, let these seventeen minutes stretch in a supernatural way. As a matter of fact, please stop the clock, Lord. You've done it before, and I really need a good nap.

Raindrops were rolling down the den windows. The wind was blowing. Branches were swaying. Leaves were falling. The house let out an occasional "creak." I read two lines and fell fast asleep. Unfortunately, the Lord did not answer my prayer.

In what seemed like a minute later, the front door flew open with an announcement from my gregarious nine-year-old-son, Jordan. "Maaaaaaa! We're ho-o-ome!" I can always count on the little guy for a bear hug.

My daughter Paris has turned into a sophisticated sixth grader. She came to the edge of my personal space and whispered, "Hello, Mother," without making eye contact. Following closely behind, as is her lot in life, was my baby. Capri has finally turned six after what seemed like an eternity of being stuck at five and a half.

Along with energizing me and bringing our home much joy and laughter, Capri makes me even more tired than rainy days and Mondays. She knows what she wants and when she wants it. She doesn't let the big kids pull anything over on her. She chooses items at the supermarket and places them in the cart. (The older two would never have tried this.) She refuses to kiss relatives or friends on command. She is the one with a heavy Brooklyn accent, even though she left New York when she was two. And with that accent, she tells people what she thinks of them and how they really smell.

This is the child that has me rereading James Dobson's bestsellers. That particular day was like all others in that she dropped her coat in the foyer, her backpack in the entrance of the den, and her well-guarded, handheld artwork on the coffee table. She shunned her big-girl persona and reverted to playing baby of the house: "Mommy, Mommy, I missed you Mommy." Her thumb went into her mouth and she climbed on top of me. We cuddled for a blissful moment. Her thumb got a brief reprieve.

"Mommy, I do not like this weather."

"Me either."

"Are you sick or something?"

"No, Mommy's just a little tired."

"Did you exercise or something?"

"No, I'm too old to exercise."

"How old are you, anyway?"

"I'm thirty years old."

"No, you're not! You're forty-one! Faker!"

"If you know my age, why did you ask?"

"I was just checking to see if you knew."

"Mommies know a lot of things."

"Will you be dead for my wedding?"

"No, I plan to be there. Daddy might be dead. He's older than me."

"How old will you be when I'm forty?"

"I'll be seventy-five."

"How old will you be when I'm fifteen?"

"I'll be fifty." (ouch)

"How will I find you when I get to heaven?"

"I'll be in the Italian restaurant at the all-you-can-eat buffet."

"Mommy. I'm serious."

"Oh, honey, you won't have to worry about that. Jesus will show you where I am."

"How does God put people in hell? Does he drop 'em in?"

"Well, no. It's kind of hard to explain, but you don't need to worry because you're going to heaven."

"Does God have a list of who's going to heaven?"

"Yes, as a matter of fact, he does."

"What if you're on the list, and you do a bad thing?"

"If you are really sorry for your sin, God can see into your heart and he will forgive you. The thief on the cross didn't act very nice and he did a lot of bad things, but he is in heaven because he was very, very sorry and he believed in Jesus."

"Do we have to brush teeth in heaven?"

"No, we'll all have dentures that don't wear out."

"Do we have to take showers?"

"Nope. Everybody there smells good forever."

"I'm gonna like heaven. Just make sure you're right there when I get there."

She poked her tiny pointer finger close to my nose and said with rhythm, authority, and a semi-threatening tone, "Be at the gate and don't be late! You got it?"

I pulled her forty-pound frame closer toward me and held her tight. "I got it."

Homework time and dinnertime and bath time and devotion time and tuck-in time all came and went on that rainy Monday night. As I lay my own body down to sleep, I thought about heaven and how far away it seems. I thought about the people I love who have found their eternal rest. I thought of those who look for rest everywhere except in God. I pondered how all that I believe in and all that I base my life on leads to a goal, a prize, a finish line called heaven.

I'm told eternity is a very long time and that heaven is a very wonderful place. My deepest desire for my family, my friends, my neighbors, and ultimately for the global community, isn't really any different than that of my six-year-old. Be at the gate and don't be late. It's a finish line you'll want to be sure to cross.

———————

He will wipe every tear from their eyes. There will be no more death or mourning or crying or pain, for the old order of things has passed away. (Revelation 21:4)

SECTION *Five*

The COMFORT
OF A MOTHER

SOMEONE TO COME HOME TO

MARGARET JENSEN

from *First We Have Coffee*

Mama closed the door to her office and slumped to her knees in utter exhaustion. "I can't go on! I can't!" She wept into her folded arms, "My strength is gone! I cry to Thee, oh Lord, for Thou alone are my strong tower. Even Moses cried to You when the task was too great. You said, 'Moses, there is a place by Me, in the cleft of the rock, until the storm passes by.' I know You are Creator of heaven and earth—a God of miracles. Today I ask one special thing: Please send me a cook."

Homesick for her beloved land, the cook had left suddenly for Norway. In addition to all the administrative duties, Mama had to fill the void in the kitchen, cooking for 45 children.

Days, months, and years were speeding out of control, like a train that wouldn't stop. She tried to get off someplace, to acclimate herself to life on solid ground, but the train moved faster.

She arose quietly and opened her Bible: "They that wait upon the Lord shall renew their strength; they shall mount up with wings as eagles; they shall run, and not be weary; and they shall walk, and not faint" (Isaiah 40:31). "Come unto me, all ye that labour and are heavy laden, and I will give you rest" (Matthew 11:28).

As she did every day, Mama spoke to the silent pictures of her own children. All but Jeanelle had flown Mama's nest; Mama prayed for us across the miles. "Oh, my children, God is your refuge. He never fails." Turning the pages of her Bible, she read again, "I will never leave thee, nor forsake thee," and "I can do all things through Christ which strengtheneth me."

Quietly, softly, the Word became a living sound. By rote Mama repeated verses that floated randomly through her mind. "The Lord is my light and my salvation." "God is my refuge and strength." "Casting all your care upon Him for He careth for you."

The quiet was broken by an insistent knock at the door. "There is someone to see you, Mrs. Tweten."

Pausing for a moment, Mama breathed in the strength that God had renewed in her. She allowed the mantle of love to cover her with the "peace that passeth understanding." She closed her Bible and went to the door to greet her visitor.

Before her stood a plump Norwegian woman. In broken English she said, "I don't speak much English, but I need vork. Could you use a cook?"

"Before they call, I will answer," came to Mama's mind.

A few days later a distraught mother with six children came to Mama's waiting room. "Please take my children!" she pleaded. Huddled in silent fear, the children clung to their mother's skirt. "I can't go on! My strength is gone, and I can't manage another day!"

"Come, let's have a cup of coffee, and we can talk," comforted Mama. The children ate cookies apprehensively and watched quietly. "I recently said those same words," continued Mama, "but God gave me an answer. Let me read it to you. We'll pray together and ask God for a miracle. In the meantime, just hold on for one week. Keep your children with you. They need you. Trust Him for a miracle, and see what happens."

"Yes, I'll try a little longer," she answered. She gathered her children and returned home.

Weeks passed before Mama remembered the distraught woman and decided to visit her. When she saw the abandoned rat-infested basement flat she had sent the woman back to, she wept. No wonder the woman had given up—or had she? Where could she have gone?

An elderly man, leaning on a cane, called to Mama, "Hey, lady, they ain't here no more. She was going to put her kids in an orphanage and then she decided to try one more week. You know something? The old man got a real good job in Chicago and came for her and the kids. He had a nice clean flat— an upstairs flat with steam heat—waiting for them. It happened so fast, lady. In a week they were gone."

"Oh, thank you, sir, and God bless you. I'll come back to visit you." Mama remembered, "Who comforteth us in all our tribulation, that we may be able to comfort them which are in any trouble, by the comfort wherewith we ourselves are comforted of God" (2 Corinthians 1:4).

Returning to the children's home, Mama opened the door humming softly one of her favorite songs, "Be not dismayed whate'er betide; God will take care of you."

The nurse met Mama at the door. "Bobby is sick."

"Not Bobby!"

Impulsively, Mama picked a flower from the patch by the porch and took it to Bobby. His fever was high, and he breathed heavily. Within moments Dr. Fanta was on his way, and four-year-old Bobby was taken to Lutheran Deaconess Hospital. In his hands he clutched the wilting flower.

Mama went with him, but she couldn't stay away from the home all day.

"I'll be back, Bobby. I have work to do, but I'll be back to see you later. Just hold the flower and let it remind you that I'll be back." With these words Mama left to attend to administrative duties. In the meantime the nurses talked amongst themselves, "Too bad his mother is dead," commented one. "He has no one, you know."

Half asleep, Bobby overheard the words that floated through the door. "His mother is dead, he has no one." He drifted into a semi-coma, and some time passed before he was fully conscious again. Suddenly he sat up. The first thing he saw was Mama holding fresh flowers.

"You're not dead! You're not dead!"

"No, Bobby. Of course I'm not dead. Of course I am your mother. You'll always belong to me, no matter how old you get."

He fell asleep, clutching a fresh flower, and Mama sat beside him, praying and singing.

"Everyone needs to belong to someone," Mama thought. "God says we belong to Him. He bought us with His Son."

One day when the "big boys," 14- to 16-year-olds, were helping in the kitchen, Mama overheard their conversation: "When we become eighteen we have to leave the home," one boy said.

Another commented, "I'm going into the service." A third boy said, "I'm going to college."

The fourth boy was quiet.

"What are you thinking about?" Mama asked Tommy.

"Mother, whom do we come home to when we go away?"

"Boys, you can come home to me!"

"Will you always be here?"

"You can come home, wherever I am."

The boys finished their chores. With an impulsive hug, Tommy reassured himself, "We have to have someone to come home to."

Mama remembered Psalm 90:1: "[God is] our dwelling place [our Home] in all generations."

We all have Someone to come home to.

ADVENTURING WITH GOD

PENELOPE J. STOKES

from Beside a Quiet Stream: Words of Hope for Weary Hearts

My mother had a unique perspective about situations that didn't go quite right. On family vacations, if we got lost and drove fifty miles on the wrong road, she would say, "Well, it's an adventure." If the charming lakeside cabin we had rented turned out to be a broken-down, spider-infested shack on the banks of a moss-covered lagoon, she'd say—after calling for reservations at the nearest motel, of course—"Well, it's an adventure."

As Christians, we might do well to adopt that attitude toward the lifetime journey we're taking with God. Circumstances don't always turn out, up close and personal, the way they looked on the brochure. Disappointments come, right along with the wonderful surprises. Difficulties catch us off guard. But we learn. We grow. We change. And when we look back, we can usually say that the situations that brought pain also brought new insight, deeper understanding, a closer relationship with God.

Attitude is everything. We can see life as a test to be endured, a dismal maze that keeps us going around in circles. Or we can look beyond the difficulties and see the adventure.

Adventure is never without its danger—in part, that's what makes it exciting, exhilarating, challenging. We stretch ourselves, go beyond the limitations that we've always accepted, find out what we're made of. And whether we succeed or fail, we become something more than we thought we were in the first place.

The disciples discovered what it meant to adventure with Jesus. It wasn't all thrills and miracles—curing lepers, watching the blind regain their sight, the lame walk, and the deaf hear. Sometimes Jesus fed five thousand with a little boy's lunch; sometimes his disciples were so hungry they gleaned the fields along the way. The crowds gathered around, sometimes listening, sometimes threatening their lives. The same people who shouted "Hosanna!" one day yelled "Crucify him!" the next. But even when the crucifixion had been accomplished and evil seemed to have won the day, the adventure wasn't over.

Because adventuring with God isn't about circumstances—it's about character. What happens to us doesn't matter nearly as much as what happens in us. The ups and downs of life, our personal crucifixions and resurrections, our victories and defeats, our stormy days and serene sunsets, all work in concert to make us into the people God has created us to be.

We don't always know where we're going, but we set our sails to the wind. Journeying with God is an adventure that will last a lifetime—and beyond.

AS A LITTLE CHILD

TRACIE PETERSON

from *The Eyes of the Heart*

At my son's first Christmas, we gifted him with a stuffed animal that he was to later dub "Kitty." The only "problem," and it never really was that much of a problem, was that this was a stuffed bear and not a cat.

The bear was fluffy and full faced, however, and my son was convinced that this was a kitty. Kitty soon became a vested member of the family. He and my son, Erik, shared the strangest relationship of love that I've ever witnessed between a child and a toy.

When Erik would be upset and crying, he would pause in mid-cry to cry for Kitty. We witnessed this in disbelief the first couple of times. Erik would cry, tears streaming down his face. Then Kitty would cry, Erik holding him up, saying, "Mew, mew, mew."

Kitty became a companion extraordinaire. Kitty traveled when Erik traveled. If Erik went to Grandma and Grandpa's house, Kitty went there as well. If Erik went to the zoo, Kitty went to the zoo.

Kitty has traveled to more states (even one foreign country) than most people I know. I don't want to tell you how many frequent-flyer miles Kitty has logged, but let's just say he can go first-class to Europe anytime he wants.

Kitty started out fluffy and clean, all gray and white with a sweet, contented, Buddha-like smile on his face. He was stuffed full and sat up by himself in regal form. Twelve years later, however, he's had the stuffing loved right out of him. His fur has been loved off, and he's undergone many rounds of plastic surgery.

One such surgery came as a result of my son's having taken Kitty to spend the night with some family friends. Erik hadn't experienced overnights on his own before, so he took Kitty with him. After all, if you're going to be in a strange place, it's best to have a friend along. We warned him that something could happen to Kitty. He could get misplaced or damaged, but our son wouldn't take no for answer. If Kitty couldn't go, he wouldn't go.

What neither Kitty nor my son expected was Dumplin'. Dumplin' is a sweetheart of a golden retriever. Generally mild-mannered and a friend to all, nobody thought anything about Dumplin' and Kitty spending time together. But as is often the case, tragedy came in the unexpected.

I was on my way to bed when the phone call came. A very subdued little boy spoke to me from the other end of the line. "Mom?" he said, his voice slightly quivering. "There's been an accident."

Of course, my mind ran rampant. Had he broken his arm? Cut his foot? Was it some other type of accident—you know, the embarrassing bathroom kind?

"What's happened?" I asked, trying my best to keep my voice from sounding too anxious.

"Dumplin' chewed off Kitty's nose." His voice broke, but he recovered quickly. "Mom, come get us."

My friend came on the line about that time and explained that Kitty and Dumplin' had been left alone to share amiable company, when they apparently had some sort of disagreement. We believe it might have been theological or political, but, of course, we can't prove it. The disagreement resulted in Dumplin's chewing off not only the nose but a good portion of the face. Stuffing was pouring out, and the nose was missing.

My heart went out to my son. I knew what he was feeling. He was shocked and mortified that this had happened, but he was also heartbroken because his best friend was wounded.

"You don't have to come get him," my friend said. "After all, it is after midnight."

"No, that's all right," I replied, knowing that my son would never sleep a wink so long as Kitty was in misery.

I left my daughters and husband at home and set out on the rescue mission. As I drove across town, I tried to think of how I would deal with the situation. I didn't want to baby my son too much. It was bad enough that I was giving in to getting him in the middle of the night. I knew the psychologists would probably never agree with my actions, but I didn't care. I heard the brokenness in my little boy's voice. I had to be there for him, to prove that I was never more than a phone call away.

When I arrived at my friend's house, the place was in mild chaos. The boys all met me at the door. Erik fought hard to keep from crying as he hugged me close and held up the plastic-wrapped bundle.

"He's . . . in here," Erik whispered stoically.

"Erik said you would fix Kitty tonight," one of the boys said.

Another one chimed in, "But we told him you wouldn't 'cause it's so late, and Kitty is so torn up."

My son looked to me, his expression full of faith. "I told them you could fix Kitty," Erik said, as if to answer all their doubts. "I told them you knew it was important, and you would do it for me."

There is nothing in this world that would have kept me from fixing that poor ragged bear for my son. His faith in me was overwhelming. I could have broken both arms on the way back home, and still I would have found a way to stitch Kitty back together. I wanted very much for my son to believe—to have faith—in my love for him.

We turned to go, and my girlfriend apologized. "Oh, by the way, we couldn't find Kitty's nose."

I nodded, seeing the impossibility of it all. I don't think I have ever prayed harder for the skills of a surgeon than I did that night. Once we were in the car, my son broke into tears and leaned against me, heartbroken.

"I hate that dog!" he sobbed.

"No, don't hate Dumplin'," I said. "She's just a dog, and she didn't know any better. She didn't do this to be mean to Kitty or to you."

Erik calmed down a bit. "You will fix Kitty, won't you?"

I heard the need for reassurance in his voice. "I'll do what I can."

"And you'll do it when we get home?"

"Absolutely," I promised.

Erik leaned back and nodded. He wiped his tears away. "I told them you would."

I don't know about you, but I want that kind of faith. I want to bring my broken toys to God and know without the slightest hint of doubt that He will fix them. I want to be able to say with as much confidence as a small boy that my Father would take care of the matter—and take care of it in a manner that would befit my need.

In Mark 10:14–15, Jesus is rather indignant with his disciples. People are bringing their children to him for a blessing—a touch, but the disciples see this as a nuisance. Jesus tells them, "Let the little children come to me, and do not hinder them, for the kingdom of God belongs to such as these. I tell you the truth, anyone who will not receive the kingdom of God like a little child will never enter it."

These verses bless my heart. Maybe it's because I always feel rather childlike and intimidated by great theological minds with multiple initials following their names. Maybe it's because I've always known that God is the Creator of the universe, but I've never cared about how He did it beyond His speaking it into existence. And maybe it's because when I'm faced with difficult situations, I go running to the lap of my heavenly Father first, and that's where I want to stay.

My heart often feels very much like a child's heart. The new and wondrous things of this earth easily excite me. And I trust my Father in heaven to provide what I need, when I need it, before I even know I need it.

Does this mean I've never had any doubts? Certainly not! Does it mean that I've never questioned God about bad situations? Nope. Does it mean that I'm always in right accordance with my Father because of some great faith within me? Absolutely not!

It simply means that after years and years of taking my needs to God, He has never failed to stay up late enough to fix them. He's never denied me in front of my friends. He's never turned away, saying, "Well, you knew there was a possibility of this happening; now deal with it on your own."

So how do we receive the kingdom of God like a little child?

As I stitched on Kitty's broken face, with tiny dedicated stitches, I couldn't help but think of God and how His love for me was even greater than my love for Erik. How He desires to heal our wounds, comfort us in times of pain, and fix the wrongs. I wanted to display my trust in God with the same overwhelming confidence that my son had displayed trust in me.

I finished Kitty's surgery with a tremendous sense of accomplishment. He was a little worse for the wear, but not much. He was still smiling with his renewed simplistic smile, and he now had a new nose, brown instead of black. But most important, he was still Kitty.

Erik had waited for me in the living room, and when I entered the room, I felt like a doctor exiting surgery. And truly, that's what I was. Erik looked up at me with no less hope than that of a parent awaiting word on his injured child.

I held up Kitty.

Erik smiled and took his worn bear in hand. "Thanks, Mom," he said, hugging me tight. "I knew you could do it."

The look on his face said it all. The trust was evident. There was no room for a single thread of doubt.

O God, I want the faith of an eight-year-old.

MOTHER AS COMFORTER

MARIE CHAPIAN

from *Mothers & Daughters*

When I was five we lived in an apartment in St. Paul, Minnesota. There was a scrubby patch of grass in the front, flagstone leading up to the building and trees that walled us in from the warmth and light of the sun. My little room was at the side of the hall across from the bathroom, and it had one window facing north and a closet. The window looked out at a fence, and in my closet I imagined a secret kingdom of queens and kings and princes and princesses behind my dresses and my shoes. I don't ever remember the sun shining in that room, but it was my room and that made it more magical and special than any other place in all the world. It was my happy little space where all my treasures were kept.

When I was five I became ill with pneumonia and the room became filled with sickness. Chicken pox, measles, pneumonia—all happened in that room. Pneumonia was the worst. My mother covered me with sheet tents and bathed me in steam. She wrapped me in towels and spooned hot broth into my mouth. She sat beside me and watched as the hot kettle puffed steam into my tent, just in case I moved and accidentally tipped it. She placed the radio beside me so I could hear music. I remember the sounds of my mother moving about in my little room. I remember my mother's touch, her smoothing my hair. I remember knowing that her hands did everything right. She fixed my tent. She made the steam so I would get well again and be able to breathe without coughing. She washed my cheeks with a cold cloth. I was not afraid. I didn't worry. (Those feelings I learned much later in life for far less serious reasons.) As a child of five with my mother hovering over me, I was unafraid. I didn't know she was fighting for the life of her daughter, determined to conquer the demons of pneumonia and death with her tools of home remedies, love and bone determination.

111

Nearly twenty years later I came down with pneumonia again. It was in New York City, and I lay in a hospital bed. I received antibiotics, there was an oxygen tent, electric steam and heating pads, but the loving hands and sounds of my mother moving in the room were not there.

My little girls and their daddy came each day and waited outside beneath my hospital window for a glimpse of me. And so every day I could look down and see the people who loved me, so tiny and far away in the color and energy of the outside world. Even if it was only a twenty-second glimpse, a weak grasping of my fingers against the windowpane, I saw them, my family.

My mother had no sophisticated equipment, no antibiotics to heal me when I was five, yet I became well. And years later in that hospital room, feverish and choking for air and life, my family waving and smiling at me, I remembered that Jesus told us love conquers all. I became well.

There have been other times in my life when I have been gasping and choking for breath, but not with physical illness. Perhaps the cares and stresses of life were crushing or my heart was broken, and I longed for the quiet, confident sounds of a loving mother in the room. She wasn't there.

These moments when nobody knows you're dying except you—nobody else is sitting up with you as you cough on your troubles in the night—these are the moments to reach out for the mother-love of Christ. We Christians don't have a problem seeing God as the Father figure, but we often forget that He is all in all. If mankind is created in His image, that includes women, and to view Him only as paternal is to limit Him. He is maternal as well.

———

In the day when God created man, He made him in the likeness of God. He created them male and female, and He blessed them and named them Man in the day when they were created. (Genesis 5:1b–2)

I have learned to recognize the Lord's maternal loving-kindness as well as His paternal power and glory. He considers His daughters to be "as corner pillars fashioned as for a palace" (Psalm 144:12b), and when I am weak with hurts too great for me, I call upon my Holy Father-Mother God and Savior who sustains all who fall, and raises up all who are bowed down (Psalm 145:14); I reach out to Him who is gracious and merciful, slow to anger and great in lovingkindness; He is our Lord who is good to all, whose mercies are over all His works (Psalm 145:8–9).

THE GREAT COVERER

CANDY ARRINGTON

At some point over the years, we dubbed Mama "The Great Coverer." The title is fitting because she seems to have an internal drive to ensure the warmth and comfort of anyone in her sphere of influence. It is not unusual for a family member, a friend, a stranger, who is reclining, even though briefly, to awake covered with an afghan, blanket, or an occasional beach towel. Mama's comfort-giving mechanism requires her to cover at every possible opportunity. For Mama, giving comfort is synonymous with love.

Mama's covering isn't limited to those who are dozing. For years she carried sweaters in the trunk of her car for my children—just in case. The trunk was most often popped open and sweaters retrieved before entering a local restaurant that served frosty confections. As the children began to shiver while consuming their treats in "air-conditioned comfort," the little sweaters appeared from her lap to swallow chill-bumped arms. To my knowledge those little sweaters still travel in her trunk—just in case. The children are now in their teens.

When I was a child, we attended every Friday night high school football game. To my embarrassment, Mama always trailed into the stadium with scratchy wool army blankets in tow. As cheerleaders flipped, titans clashed, bands piped, and nippy autumn air swirled, Mama spread the woolen wraps around us and passed steaming cups of hot chocolate poured from a plaid thermos.

On one occasion, when the temperatures were well below freezing, she produced large plastic leaf bags and insisted we stand in them and cinch the drawstrings around our waists. One unsuspecting father and son in front of us came under her ministrations when she determined they were armed only with sweaters for the evening and insisted they don trash bags also. You can imagine the questioning looks from our stand-mates.

The county fair was a treat with its barns of animal smells, house of flowers, cotton candy hawkers, and glittering midway. I remember the swish of the corduroy pants Mama insisted I wear under my jumper to ward off chilly evening temperatures. A sweater topped by a jacket, hat, and gloves completed the ensemble, and I was toasty warm for the evening's excitement.

Although Mama's covering efforts could be a source of annoyance, they were always done with the best intentions. Perhaps her desire to cover was a result of her being the oldest of five children and feeling the need to take care of her siblings. Or, possibly, the effects of the Great Depression left an indelible mark. Whatever the reasons, Mama never wants anyone to be uncomfortable.

God's love is similar to that of "The Great Coverer." His love enfolds us in a blanket of protection and encouragement when trouble and uncertainty buffet our lives. His peace spreads comfort over all life's trials. The sin-cover of the blood of Jesus brings us into right standing with the Father and allows us to call him Abba—Daddy.

Somehow I imagine when Mama enters heaven, God will be waiting, ready to swathe her in the embrace of his everlasting arms. And I wouldn't be surprised if "The Great Coverer" and "The Great Comforter" spend eternity in a never-ending hug.

THE DISTANT RUMBLE

SHEILA WALSH

from *Honestly*

M y mother was a strong link in a long line of godly women. She knew a little of what was happening to me, but I knew I had to try to prepare her for how I looked. I had dropped about twenty pounds, a significant loss on my five-foot-four-inch frame.

My mother had seen bad times herself. When I was four years old, my father had suffered a brain thrombosis. He died a year later. His absence was felt every day, but my mother filled our home with her spirit, her understanding, her faith, her love of life, and her wonderful sense of humor.

She had always been there for me. When I came home from school, I knew she would be waiting to hear all about it. When I was eleven, I asked my mother if she would pray with me. I wanted to make a personal commitment to beginning my own journey with God, even though I had no idea where that road would lead.

For a while I wanted to be a missionary in India. I don't think I experienced a specific call to the mission field; it just sounded like the ultimate sacrifice. I hated to be away from home, and I was petrified of snakes and spiders, so I figured such a visible, measurable sign would show God that I loved him.

During my teenage years I remember watching as a friend from church rebelled for a time, drinking and partying. The impact that had on me was a fierce commitment to be different. I would walk along the beach after church or youth group meetings and pray out loud, calling on the stars to be my witnesses that I would never let God down, that he could always count on me. That prayer became a theme for my life.

At nineteen I left Scotland to study at London Bible College. I thought I had arrived in paradise. They say that when you are tired of London, you are tired of life. Well, I was wide awake. I went to the ballet, the opera, the theater, all on student tickets. My seat might have been far away, but I was right there on that stage—I never missed a note. Though I drank in the atmosphere daily, I never forgot for a moment why I was there: I wanted to know God's purpose for my life. Still seeing the mission field as a woman's "most committed option," I joined so many mission prayer groups I often had to let someone else pray first to remind me what group I was in. (It's Thursday, it must be Africa!)

As time passed I began to see that there was a mission field right on my doorstep. As part of our evangelistic practicum I would visit other college campuses on the weekends. For me this was much more than a course I needed for credit. Some of my friends and I put a band together, and as I stood in college gymnasiums singing about my relationship with God, I knew I had found what I was created for.

When I graduated, I let the boat for Calcutta sail past, and I joined Youth For Christ as a staff member, traveling across Europe and the United Kingdom, singing and speaking the Gospel. *Here am I, a musical evangelist,* I often thought. *Lord, send me wherever you can use me.*

And he did. For the next ten years, I traveled all over the world, gaining an increasingly loyal audience. I released several record albums and served as host for a BBC TV show featuring contemporary Christian and traditional black gospel music.

The problem was, somewhere along the road I had lost my way. Somewhere I'd lost the joy of my salvation and my calling. I chose to carry my calling rather than let the One who called me carry *me.*

Now I looked out of the plane as we circled the green fields outside of Glasgow. I was home.

As I stood in the early morning chill at the airport, I drank in the sounds and the accents as I waited for my suitcase, the wonderfully comforting sounds that had surrounded me as a child.

I picked up a car and drove fifty minutes south to my mother's house in Ayr. I love that drive. The roads wind narrowly along green fields, over hills, past herds of the black and white cattle this area is known for. There is a point in the journey where you can first see the ocean. I look for it every time. When

I see it, I know I am almost home. The Ayrshire coastline is so beautiful: sandy beaches, cliff tops that hold the remains of an old castle, seagulls, and salty spray.

I drove up the familiar road and parked outside my mother's gate. I knew she would be watching for me, as she always did, kettle boiling, ready to make that first cup of real tea.

When she saw me, she started to cry. I guess I looked worse than I realized. I had asked her not to tell people what was happening in my life; it still seemed too unbelievable to me. But over that first cup of tea, she said; "If you don't want anyone to know that something's wrong, Sheila, you had better stay home all week, because anyone who knows you will be shocked when they see you."

I began to eat when I was home. Mom made all my favorites: minced beef with peas in it, mashed potatoes, home-baked cakes, and piping hot tea. It was so good to be there. Our family pastor, an Irish man, came and spent some time with me and prayed for me. His gentle words and strong prayers were like rain in the desert.

My sister and her husband and their two little boys live in Ayr too. One night when I was at their house, David, their older boy, presented me with a chocolate cake he had baked himself. "You look ill, Aunt Sheila," he said. "This will help."

Mom and I walked along the ocean and drove over the hills and talked and talked and talked some more. I told her what a failure I felt like, that I was afraid I was letting her down. But that isn't how my mother saw me. She hugged me and wept with me. She told me to hold on to the Lord, to take each day as it came, and that she loved me. I would need her words for the days that lay ahead.

SECTION *Six*

The STRENGTH OF A MOTHER

FORK IN THE ROAD

PHIL CALLAWAY

from *I Used to Have Answers, Now I Have Kids*

I have been a husband for nearly ten years now, so needless to say I know virtually everything there is to know about my wife's needs. For instance, I know that she can get by without sleep for three days and three nights, but definitely not without chocolate. I also know that she needs flowers, nurturing, romance, protection, a listening ear, clean laundry, and clothes that fit. Whereas, my basic needs are . . . well, pizza.

It is a quarter to five right now and I am sitting at my desk thinking about my need for pizza. It's been one of those days at the office. A computer blip swallowed half the morning's work, and nothing went right after that. I had no time for lunch. Deadlines loom. Reports beckon. And my stomach growls. It is saying, "Hey, give us pizza. We need pizza."

As the clock struggles toward 5 P.M., however, the growling is muffled in visions of home. Dinner will be store-bought Coke and homemade pizza. Toppings will include large hunks of pepperoni, layers of ham, and enough cheese to blanket Switzerland. The crust will be light yet crunchy, flavored with a generous pinch of oregano. When I arrive, Ramona will be waiting at the door, her hair permed, her lips pursed. The children will be setting the table, newly washed smiles gracing each of their faces. "Hi Daddy!" they will say in unison. "We sure missed you."

Following dinner, the children will beg to be put to bed early. "We want you and Mom to have some time alone," they will say. "You've probably had a tough day."

As I park the car, however, I realize that something has gone terribly wrong. For one thing, half the neighborhood is in our yard. As I enter the house, I find the other half. They are rifling through our refrigerator. In the kitchen Ramona is bent over the dishwasher, cleaning out the last of the silverware. The table is piled high with laundry, and the stove holds not even a hint of supper.

Several times in my life I have said things people did not appreciate. This is one of those times.

"So what's for supper?" I ask. "Roast beef?" There is silence.

I sit down before the laundry and make an even bigger mistake. "So," I say, "what did you do today?"

Sometimes my wife moves very quickly. This is one of those times. Ramona stands up straight, brandishing a sharp fork.

"What did I do today?"

She walks swiftly across the room—still holding the fork.

"WHAT DID I DO TODAY?"

She hands me a piece of paper. A piece of paper women everywhere should own. Then she stands over me as I read it.

WHAT I DID TODAY

3:21 A.M.—Woke up. Took Jeffrey to bathroom.

3:31 A.M.—Woke up. Took Jeffrey back to bed.

3:46 A.M.—Got you to quit snoring.

3:49 A.M.—Went to sleep.

5:11 A.M.—Woke up. Took Jeffrey to bathroom.

6:50 A.M.—Alarm went off. Mentally reviewed all I had to do today.

7:00 A.M.—Alarm went off.

7:10 A.M.—Alarm went off. Contemplated doing something violent to alarm clock.

7:19 A.M.—Got up. Got dressed. Made bed. Warned Stephen.

7:20 A.M.—Warned Stephen.

7:21 A.M.—Spanked Stephen. Held Stephen. Prayed with Stephen.

7:29 A.M.—Fed boys a breakfast consisting of Cheerios, orange juice, and something that resembled toast. Scolded Jeffrey for mixing them.

7:35 A.M.—Woke Rachael.

7:48 A.M.—Had devotions.

7:49 A.M.—Made Stephen's lunch. Tried to answer Jeffrey's question "Why does God need people?" Warned Stephen.

8:01 A.M.—Woke Rachael.

8:02 A.M.—Started laundry.

8:03 A.M.—Took rocks out of washing machine.

8:04 A.M.—Started laundry.

8:13 A.M.—Planned grocery list. Tried to answer Jeffrey's question "Why do we need God?"

8:29 A.M.—Woke Rachael (third time).

8:30 A.M.—Helped Stephen with homework.

8:31 A.M.—Sent Stephen to school. Told him to remember his lunch.

8:32 A.M.—Had breakfast with Rachael. Porridge.

Rest of morning—Took Stephen's lunch to him. Returned library books. Explained why a cover was missing. Mailed letters. Bought groceries. Shut TV off. Planned birthday party. Cleaned house. Wiped noses. Wiped windows. Wiped bottoms. Shut TV off. Cleaned spaghetti out of carpet. Cut bite marks off the cheese. Made owl-shaped sandwiches.

12:35 P.M.—Put wet clothes in dryer.

12:38 P.M.—Sat down to rest.

12:39 P.M.—Scolded Jeffrey. Helped him put clothes back in dryer.

12:45 P.M.—Agreed to babysit for a friend.

Cut tree sap out of Rachael's hair. Regretted babysitting decision. Killed assorted insects. Read to the kids. Clipped ten fingernails. Sent kids outside. Unpacked groceries. Watered plants. Swept floor. Picked watermelon seeds off linoleum. Read to the kids.

3:43 P.M.—Stephen came home. Warned Stephen.

3:46 P.M.—Put Band-Aids on knees.

Organized task force to clean kitchen. Cleaned parts of house. Accepted appointment to local committee (secretary said, "You probably have extra time since you don't work"). Tried to answer Rachael's question "Why are boys and girls different?" Listened to a zillion more questions. Answered a few. Cleaned out dishwasher. Briefly considered supper. Briefly considered running away from home.

5:21 P.M.—Husband arrived looking for peace, perfection, and pizza.

I am finished reading now, but Ramona is not through. "Of course, not all my days go this smoothly," she says, still clutching the fork.

"Any questions?"

Often when Ramona and I are at public gatherings, she is asked The Question: "Do you work?" I'm glad she is not holding a fork at this point. Sometimes I wish she'd say, "Actually I work days, nights, and weekends. How about you?" But she doesn't. She's a kind woman. She practices what I preach. Once, however, she confided that she wishes she had the eloquence to respond as one woman did: "I am socializing three homo sapiens in the dominant values of the Judeo-Christian tradition in order that they might be instruments for the transformation of the social order into the teleologically prescribed utopia inherent in the eschaton."

Then she would ask, "And what is it you do?"

"I'm a lawyer" just isn't all that overpowering after that.

A MOTHER'S DISCIPLINE

BIRDIE ETCHISON

Sarah, my sixth and last child, defied all rules and disciplinary measures. I was desperate for answers.

I tried reverse psychology in her younger years. She would ask for my opinion and if I said one thing, she'd do the opposite. I learned early on to suggest the opposite of what I wanted her to do. Some of the examples were ridiculously simple.

"Should I wear the pink or the blue top?"

"Oh, by all means wear the pink."

Five minutes later she'd be sporting the blue.

When she was little, we'd have what we called Family Altar each evening. We'd bought a book of Bible stories and every night read a different story. There were questions at the end. Sarah never answered one, while her brother, twenty months older, wriggled with excitement. He knew the answers to every question.

All through her school years, Sarah disrupted . . . something. When she entered first grade, she was caught writing *love* in huge letters on a school wall. She could not understand why the teacher was upset.

"But love is a good word," she argued.

No matter what the rule might be, she fought it. We tried different forms of discipline, thinking something would work. I had treated all my children the same, but my methods did not work for Sarah. I needed some answers.

Out of desperation we attended a group therapy led by Margaret, a former teacher and Christian counselor. Tears flooded my eyes as I listened while others talked about their difficulties with discipline. It was comforting to know I wasn't the only one with an obstinate child. Finally, after eleven years of constant chaos, we'd found an answer to our prayers. I went home fortified for the week to come.

"When you need to set down a rule, preface it with this statement: 'I know you are going to be angry about this, so I give you ten minutes to throw a fit.'"

Strange, but when Sarah was given permission to protest, she didn't do it.

Another rule: Since Sarah was the type of child who badgered, she could either wear me down, and she knew it, or I'd be so angry, I'd start yelling.

"Go into a room and go about your business," Margaret suggested, "and when she starts begging, pretend you don't hear. Do not say one word. Mothers tend to preach, and kids just tune you out."

This rule worked as well.

Then we moved. With my older children raised, it was just Sarah and me in new surroundings. She began high school and thrived on her newfound popularity in a smaller school.

Sarah faced the same rules, but she still fought to get her own way. My heart was heavy, as it seemed to be a losing battle. One night she wanted to attend a football game that was a three-hour drive away. It was a school night, and I refused to let her go. How could I let her ride in a car with a driver I did not know? Nor should she be out that late on a school night.

She begged, cried, and insisted, but I continued to say no.

Finally, she grabbed her jacket and purse and started off up the road toward the main highway. She was going to go in spite of what I said.

I grabbed the keys and started after her in the car. She'd already reached the highway when I got there.

"Get in the car, Sarah."

"No!" She marched on, head held high.

"Get in the car."

She continued to defy me, walking on in the direction of the school. I held the car at eight miles an hour, just fast enough to stay with her. "Get in the car," I repeated several times. She continued to say no.

Gripping the steering wheel, I almost gave in, but somehow I stayed the course, my mind and heart knowing I could not relent.

Finally, she yanked the car door open, plopped inside, and said, "Okay. I won't go, but I hate you. I hate you so much!"

That's fine, I wanted to say, but remembering Margaret's words, I said nothing, but drove back home.

The entire episode had lasted all of ten minutes. She was home. Safe. She refused to come into the house, but sat outside next to the fire pit, while I was inside reading a book.

That incident was the turning point in our tumultuous relationship.

Sarah is now in her twenties, and we enjoy doing things together. One day while we were shopping, she asked, "Do you remember that time you wouldn't let me go to the football game?"

"Of course."

"That was the day I knew you loved me."

"It was?"

"Yes. When I was growing up, I thought you favored Matt because he never got punished." She reached over and took my hand. "I realize now that he never argued and did what he was told. I was the rebel, wasn't I?"

"Yes, you were."

"It made me think about a lot of things that night."

I hugged her. "I'm so happy to hear you say that."

This revelation came when Sarah was twenty-five. With God's help, I had done the best job I could, but it was eleven years before I knew it had all been worth it.

I wondered later about how God must feel when his children don't listen, don't obey. He hangs in there with us anyway. His love and coaxing never stops. He doesn't give up, nor can we mothers give up on our children. The task was rough, but it was worth every tear, every prayer, every hope I had.

WHAT MOTHERS ARE FOR

ALETHEIA LEE BUTLER

The past year had been difficult on all of our friends. Momma was enduring chemotherapy for her first of three bouts with breast cancer. She ate little and was completely exhausted. I stayed home and cared for her while Dad was at work. She moved very little and usually had to be served anything she needed. Often she sat in a chair by the window and watched the world from which she had been temporarily removed.

I was thirteen but feeling thirty. That summer everything weighed heavily on my shoulders. Because of Joshua, the boy across the creek, at times I could be a child again—at least temporarily. We met in the seventh grade, and he became one of the greatest friends I have known. Our almost-diagonal backyards became the world of our imaginations. With Joshua, I could forget the fear of seeing my mother so ill and lose myself in our current adventure.

One hot summer morning he and I tackled the impossible job of convincing our stubborn flower garden to grow anything but weeds. We labored away most of the day. Momma sat just inside the door in her favorite chair, escaping the heat, but enjoying our escapades in the front yard.

Joshua and I were working with a particularly determined section of weeds when we heard footsteps behind us. He turned around first, and exhaled, "Oh no."

I knew what that meant without looking. There was only one family with children in the neighborhood that we did not play with.

"Hey, punk! What do you think you're doing?" The unpleasant visitor demanded.

"Go away. No one was bothering you."

"I want you to leave," the bully said.

"This isn't even your yard," Joshua said in a laugh that seemed to be borne of fear.

"Now you've crossed the line, and there's no one here to help you." He grabbed Joshua's shoulders and shoved him against the front porch, on top of a nail we used for hanging Christmas lights.

I was so stunned I didn't know what to do. Fortunately, Momma did. She was up, through the door, and pulling the kid off Joshua.

Joshua and I hurried inside to clean his wound. Momma shouted, "Joshua's a friend of mine. You don't come into my yard and touch one of my guests. Leave right now and never touch or speak to either of them again and never set foot in my yard. Ever!"

The boy left.

Back inside, Momma collapsed into her chair. She'd used energy she didn't have to fight off the biggest boy in school. One punch could have knocked her down, but even he respected my mom enough to do as she said.

Joshua and I exchanged looks, but no words came. He smiled in appreciation for what she had done. She smiled back. She didn't need his thanks; she was just doing her job as a mother.

As Joshua headed home to have his mother look at the cut, I sat on the sofa next to Momma's chair. The incident left me awestruck. From the look on her face I knew her little super-hero moment had left her in pain. I knew how much it took out of her because each day I watched her struggle to get out of her chair. How she leaped over small living rooms in a single bound was beyond me.

"Thank you," I whispered.

"That's what mothers are for." She put her hand on mine, and we watched the world go by.

———

This incident taught me a lesson about Christ's sacrifice for us. I'll never know how painful that instant was for my mother. Likewise, I'll never understand Christ's love in its entirety. Somehow I think that's why we are given mothers like mine—to give us a glimpse into the heart of God.

TOMMY'S TRIUMPH

KATHY IDE

F ive-year-old Tommy stood on a raised platform at the front of the chapel, his fingers wrapped comfortably around a microphone that projected his clear young voice throughout the sanctuary. "Genesis, Exodus, Leviticus, Numbers . . ."

So many eyes watching, so many ears listening intently, yet the lad continued without the slightest hesitation. "Ezra, Nehemiah, Esther, Job . . ."

Innocently unaware of the building tension in the room, Tommy spoke as calmly as if he were listing his favorite cartoon characters. "Ezekiel, Daniel, Hosea, Joel . . ." Could this child really recite the names of all sixty-six books of the Bible, in their proper order?

Parishioners leaned forward in their pews.

"Jonah, Micah, Nahum, Habakkuk . . ."

A few people stole glances at the Table of Contents in the Bibles on their laps.

Dressed in a plaid sweater vest, clip-on bow tie, dress slacks, and scuffed-up tennis shoes, Tommy stood tall, his dark brown hair meticulously combed off to the side. His voice did not waver as he spoke with the confidence of a seasoned preacher. "Zephaniah, Haggai, Zechariah, Malachi . . ."

I sat in the front pew on the edge of my seat, eyes riveted to Tommy's face, my hands clasped tightly in my lap. I had spent countless hours memorizing with my son. Every day after work, Tommy had begged me to help him with his special project. I was happy to oblige. I knew each moment I had with him was a precious gift from God.

You see, I had conceived Tommy when I was an unwed teenager. My original plan was to place my baby for adoption. But as that baby grew inside me, I became convinced that, with God's help, I could raise this child myself.

I encountered numerous struggles as a single mom. Tommy and I lived in a tiny second-floor apartment overlooking a patch of dry brown grass strewn with trash. I drove a clunky old car with inconsistent brakes and one headlight. Dinner often consisted of macaroni and cheese and corn on the cob.

What pained me most was leaving my little boy in daycare while I worked full time. But Tommy never complained. Every morning he wrapped his chubby arms around my neck and gave me a tight hug before trotting off to join his little friends. After eight hours of work and a ninety-minute drive in rush-hour traffic, I would trudge up the stairs of the daycare center. The moment Tommy saw me, his big brown eyes lit up like starlight. His lopsided smile made my spirits soar. He raced into my arms and planted a sloppy, wet kiss on my cheek. Slipping his small hand into mine, he babbled endlessly about the excitements of his day. His "I love you, Mommy" made all the struggles melt into insignificance.

And to think, I often mused, *I almost gave him up.* Life without Tommy was unthinkable now.

After some searching, I found a church whose congregation accepted me and my son without judgment. Every week Tommy came home from Sunday school singing about the "B-I-B-L-E" and how "Jesus loves me, this I know." He sang loudly of the "joy, joy, joy, joy, down in my heart." Tommy told everyone he knew about his Bible lessons and proudly recited each week's Scripture memory verse. It didn't matter whether the listeners were believers or not. Tommy's love for God simply flowed out of him as naturally as could be.

Five years old, and he's already an evangelist. And he doesn't even know it.

When Tommy asked me to help him memorize the books of the Bible, it seemed an overwhelming task. I didn't know all the names myself. I wasn't even sure how to pronounce some of them. And when would I find the time? Still, I could rarely refuse my little boy's requests, so I agreed to try.

It hadn't been easy. Several times Tommy struggled to get his mouth to form the unusual names, and his mind to recall the next one in the series. Whenever he became discouraged, he folded his hands, bowed his head, squeezed his eyes shut, and asked God to help him. As I prayed with him, I thanked the Lord for the amazing treasure he had allowed me to hold.

And yet I realized, as much as I loved my precious son, my heavenly Father loved him—and me—even more. I knew that while I cheered my little boy's accomplishments, God and his angels were cheering right along with us.

So there I sat, on the edge of that front pew, making a conscious effort to release my lower lip from between my teeth. Tommy's recital flowed effortlessly, with barely a pause between the Old Testament and the New. "Matthew, Mark, Luke, John . . ."

Shuffling feet stilled. Not even a congregational cough broke the silence.

"Galatians, Ephesians, Philippians, Colossians . . ."

Even breathing seemed to cease throughout the chapel as Tommy glided flawlessly through the home stretch. "First, Second and Third John, Jude, Revelation."

Gasps mixed with sighs as the congregation finally remembered to breathe, then thunderous applause shook the stained-glass windows.

Pastor Jenson accepted the microphone from Tommy and took a deep breath before he spoke. "When I promised a brand-new Bible to anyone who could list all the books of the Old and New Testaments," he announced, his words barely escaping past the constriction in his throat, "I never expected it to be presented to a five-year-old boy." He knelt and placed a thick leather tome into Tommy's outstretched arms.

I jumped up from my seat, unable to remain there a moment longer. I rushed onto the platform and wrapped my child in a smothering embrace. "I'm so proud of you, Tommy," I whispered. The cheers of the congregation nearly drowned out my words.

"I'm proud of you too," Tommy declared, looking up at me with unabashed admiration.

As I led my son back to the front pew, Tommy's "I love you, Mommy" made all the struggles melt into insignificance once again.

VISIBILITY

DR. PAUL BRAND
PHILIP YANCEY

from *Fearfully and Wonderfully Made*

I n India, while leprosy research consumed my time, my wife Margaret trained as an ophthalmologist and became an expert eye surgeon. Because many of the neediest people could not travel to the hospital, she and a team of helpers took a well-stocked mobile unit on monthly circuits into rural areas. On a certain date, a designated building, perhaps a school or an old rice mill, would receive a stream of Indians afflicted with runny eyes or blindness. The staff worked under crude conditions, sometimes in stifling heat, devising an assembly line of treatment. If no building was available, they would even set up portable operating tables under a banyan tree. Sometimes two doctors performed over one hundred cataract operations a day.

In 1956, Margaret's team staffed a camp for several weeks in an area of India that had been devastated by drought. Crops had failed for five years, and the wells were dry of drinking water. People straggled in from every direction, begging for food. Assuming they would have to stay at the camp to receive food, many volunteered for needless surgery—to the extent of asking that one of their eyes be removed—in order to get something to eat.

Young boys volunteered to assist at that hectic camp, and Margaret was assigned a shy, dark boy about twelve years old. He stood on a box, with an impressive but baggy hospital gown wrapped around him, charged with strict instructions to hold a three-battery flashlight so that the light beamed directly on the cornea of the patient's eye. Margaret was dubious: could a young village boy who had never watched any surgery endure the trauma of seeing people's eyes sliced open and stitched together again?

The child, however, performed his task with remarkable aplomb. During the first five operations he scrupulously followed Margaret's instructions on when to shift the angle of light, aiming the beam with a steady, confident hand. But during the sixth case he faltered. Margaret kept saying softly, "Little brother, show the light properly," which he would momentarily do, but soon it again would dangerously bob away from where she was cutting. Margaret could see that he simply could not bear to look at the eye being worked on. She stopped and asked if he was feeling well.

Tears ran down his cheeks and he stuttered, "Oh, doctor—I-I cannot look. This one, she is my mother."

Ten days later the boy's suffering was over. His mother's stitches were removed, and the team gave her eyeglasses. She first tried to blink away the dazzling light, but finally adjusted, focused, and for the first time in her life saw her son. A smile creased her face as she reached out to touch him. "My son," she said, "I thought I knew you, but today I see you." And she pulled him close to her.

Now we see but a poor reflection as in a mirror; then we shall see face to face. Now I know in part; then I shall know fully, even as I am fully known. (1 Corinthians 13:12)

TO THE POOLS OF SILOAM

WALTER WANGERIN, JR.

from *Little Lamb, Who Made Thee?*

It's been two seasons now since I saw her, but because of the tremendous respect she inspired in me (and then, as well, the pity) I can't forget her.

It picks at the back of my mind, over and over again, asking: *What does she remind me of?*

Something remarkable.

Last spring a duck entered our backyard journeying eastward, eleven little ducklings in file behind her. It was an outrageous appearing, really, since we live in the midst of the concrete city. The only waters east of us are the pools at the state hospital, four miles away, which distance is an odyssey! Between here and there are vast tracts of humanity, fences, houses, shopping malls—and immediately to our east, Bayard Park of tall trees and lawns.

Yet this duck moved her brood with a quick skill as if she knew exactly where she was going.

Buff brown generally, vague markings on her wings, a smooth pate with a cowlick at the back, she and her name were the same: blunt and unremarkable. The ducklings were puffballs with butch haircuts, obedient and happy. Big-footed, web-footed, monstrous-footed, floppy-footed, the children followed their mother as fast as drips down windowpanes, peeping, questioning, keeping together, trusting her judgment.

And she, both blunt and busy, led them into our yard, which is surrounded by a wooden palisade fence. Maybe she came this way for a rest.

But we have a dog. He rose to his feet at the astonishing sight. He raised his ears and woofed. The duck backpedaled to the wall of the house and turned eastward under the eaves' protection and waddled hard, her ducklings in mad zip behind her. But the dog is leashed and could not reach the wall. This part of the passage, at least, was safe. The next was not.

Without pausing, the buff duck spread her wings, beat the air, and barely cleared the fence, landing in the middle of Bedford Avenue between our yard and the park. There she set up a loud quacking, like a reedy woodwind: *Come! Come!*

Eleven ducklings scurried to the fence, then raced along it till they found a crack: *Plip! Plip!*—they popped through as quick as they could, but their mother must have been driven into the park. By the time they gained the wider world she had disappeared. The babies bunched in confusion, peeping, peeping grievously. One bold soul ventured down Bedford to the alley behind our yard. The others returned through the fence.

Immediately the mother was back on Bedford, the one bold child behind her, scolding the rest like an angry clarinet: *Now! Here! Come here now!*

Well, in a grateful panic ten ducklings rushed the crack in the fence, thickening there, pushing, burning with urgency, trying hard to obey their mother—

Not fast enough.

A car roared south on Bedford. Another. The duck beat retreat to the farther curb. Joggers came jogging. A knot of teenagers noticed the pretty flow of ducklings from under our fence and ran toward it. The tiny flock exploded in several directions. The mother's cries grew hectic and terrified: *Come! Come!*— her beak locked open. She raced up and down the park's edge, and there was but the one puffball following her.

The simple unity of twelve was torn apart. My city is deadly to certain kinds of families.

Five ducklings shot back and forth inside our yard now, but the hole through the fence led to roaring horrors and they couldn't persuade themselves to hazard it again—though they could hear their mother. That unremarkable duck (no!—intrepid now and most remarkable) was hurling herself in three directions, trying to compose her family in unity again: eastward she flew into the park, south toward violent alleys, then back west to the impassive fence. *Hear me now, hear me and come!* Her children were scattered. She was but one.

I saw a teenager chase one duckling. He was laughing gaily in the game. He reached down and scooped up the tiny life in his great hand and peered at it and then threw it up into the air. The baby fell crazily to the ground. The youth chased it again.

"Don't!" I yelled.

"Why not?" the kid said, straightening himself. "What? Does this duck belong to you?"

But where was the mother now? I didn't see her anywhere. And now it was bending into the later afternoon.

I poured some water into a pan and placed it by the back wall of the house for those ducklings still dithering within our yard. They huddled away from the dog. But the dog had lost interest. They crept sometimes toward the hole in the fence. Now and again a duckling looked through. Their peeping, peeping was miserable. What do you do for innocents in the city—both the wild and the child? By nightfall they had all vanished.

No, not all. I can tell you of two.

The next day we heard a scratching; in the vent pipe of our clothes dryer. I went down in the basement and disconnected the shaft and found a shivering duckling who must have fallen down from the outside opening. Perhaps it had sought cover and didn't know the cave went down so deep. It had spent a long dark night alone in its prison.

And then at church on Sunday a friend of mine said, "Weirdest thing! I saw this duck crossing highway 41—"

"What?" I cried. "A duck? Alone?"

"Well, no, not alone," said my friend. "I almost ran over her. I guess she didn't fly on account of baby ducks can't fly, and she was protecting it."

"Michelle," I said, "what do you mean *it*? How many ducklings did she have?"

"One. Just one."

There have passed two seasons, I say, since I encountered this blunt, buff duck—and still in my heart I whisper as I did then, *Godspeed* with honor and pity. *Godspeed, remarkable creature, tenacious and loving.*

And now I know what she reminds me of.

Of single-parent families in a largely indifferent world.

She reminds me of that impoverished mother (Oh, my culpable country!) who has small means to nourish and raise and protect her children. I have met that mother far too often with far too little to offer her. Mighty is her love. Illogical, absurd, and marvelous is her love for the children. And terrible is her sorrow for the loss of any one of them. The world may not enlarge her love or else diminish her sorrow. The world may in fact begrudge whatever little thing it gives her. Worse: the world can be dangerous to the family whole and to her children in particular.

But she loves. This mother knows from the beginning that the children will be chased, harassed, scorned, beaten, belittled—both by raggedy folks and by the upright and civil people of her city. She knows that one child may tumble down black shafts of a blatant disregard and another into drugs and another into crime and another into despair. From the beginning their prospects must wring her heart with a tight anxiety. She labors to give them a life for a while and some esteem and safety—and against desperate odds, marvelously, she loves.

To this one I say, *Godspeed, good parent, all the way east to the pools of Siloam and your children's maturity.*

And to the holy community of the church I say: *Help her! Surround this single parent, mother or father, with love and a service equal to her own. No: with a love equal to God's, whom you are sent to represent!*

In God's name, help her.

SECTION *Seven*

The LESSONS
OF A MOTHER

FOLLOWING TRUTH, REJECTING LIES

STORMIE OMARTIAN

from *The Power of a Praying Parent*

I n our house, our children know that while it might be possible to cut a deal on the punishment for certain infractions, if lying is part of the offense, the punishment will be swift, immediate, unpleasant, and non-negotiable. We consider telling a lie to be the worst offense because it is foundational for all other evil acts. Every sin or crime begins with someone believing or speaking a lie. Even if the lie is as simple as "I can get what I want if I lie," it paves the way for evil.

Early on, my daughter tested the water with "little white lies." But it didn't take long for her to see that the punishment for lying greatly overshadowed any possible advantage she thought she might gain as a result of telling a lie. My son, on the other hand, didn't just dabble. If he was going to tell a lie, he went for a big one.

When Christopher was seven, he was playing baseball with his friend Steven out in front of Steven's house. The ball struck the large front picture window with a loud crack, which immediately brought Steven's mother to the front door.

"Who did this?" she asked.

"I didn't do it," said Steven.

"I didn't do it," said Christopher.

"Steven, you mean to tell me you did not strike the window with this ball?" she said.

"No, I didn't," answered Steven emphatically.

"Christopher, did *you* strike the window with the ball?" she asked.

"If you saw me do it, I did it. If you didn't see me do it, I didn't do it," Christopher answered in his most matter-of-fact voice.

"I didn't see you do it," she said.

"Then I didn't do it," he replied.

When Steven's mom told us what happened, we knew we needed to deal with this matter immediately so Christopher would not think he could get away with lying.

"Christopher, someone saw everything that happened. Would you like to tell us about it?" I said, wanting his full confession and a repentant heart.

He hung his head and said, "Okay, I did it."

We had a long talk about what the Word of God says about lying. "Satan is a liar," I told him. "All the evil he does begins with a lie. People who lie believe that lying will make things better for them. But actually, it does just the opposite. That's because telling a lie means you have aligned yourself with Satan. Every time you lie you give Satan a piece of your heart. The more lies you tell, the more you give place in your heart to Satan's lying spirit, until eventually you can't stop yourself from lying. The Bible says, 'Getting treasures by a lying tongue is the fleeting fantasy of those who seek death' (Proverbs 21:6). In other words, you may *think* you're getting something by lying, but all you're really doing is bringing death into your life. The consequences of telling the truth have to be better than death. Even the punishment you receive from your parents for lying will be far more pleasant than the consequences of lying. For the Bible promises that 'A false witness will not go unpunished, and he who speaks lies will not escape' (Proverbs 19:5)."

It was quite some time after that incident before Christopher asked me who had seen him that day.

"It was God," I explained. "He saw you. I've always asked Him to reveal to me anything I need to know about you or your sister. He is the Spirit of Truth, you understand."

"Mom, that's not fair," was all he said. After that, though, on the few occasions when he told a lie, he always came to me immediately to confess it.

"I thought I better tell you before you heard it from God," he would explain.

BETWEEN NO AND YES

SHEILA WALSH

from *Living Fearlessly*

When I look closely at what Dag Hammarskjöld wrote ("For all that has been—Thanks! To all that shall be—Yes!"), there is more there than I can wrap my heart around. I believe he is saying that for every single thing that has happened in our lives, we can learn to say with confidence, even with joy, "Not my will, but yours be done." This means saying yes to the happy and beautiful gifts, but also to the child you lost, the husband who never showed up, the breast cancer, the lost opportunities, the broken dreams, the endless list of human suffering. I certainly don't believe he is suggesting that all the pain in our lives is inflicted by God to see if he can squeeze a heartbroken yes out of us. But I do embrace the mystery that, in the darkest valleys, even when saying yes will break our hearts, the Light of the world is with us, and we will come to know him, to love and trust him, in ways we never have before.

I think back to a conversation I had with a woman in Phoenix, Arizona, at a Women of Faith conference. I had been signing books and listening to a patchwork quilt of stories for about an hour. I saw her out of the corner of my eye. She was standing off to one side. She looked fragile, uncertain, alone. I smiled at her and signaled that as soon as I could I would come over to where she was. She smiled back. When the crowd thinned out, I joined her. We talked for a few moments about the events of the evening. I could tell she was carefully circling her story, searching for the internal strength to put words to the unspeakable.

"I came to Christ as a result of the death of my child," she said with tears spilling onto thin, pale cheeks.

She must have recognized the uncertainty in my eyes, and she continued to place pieces in the painful puzzle of her life story.

"I wasn't a believer when my son was born. I guess I was an agnostic. I never gave God much thought. Then he got really sick."

"What was wrong with him?" I asked.

"Oh, it was a very rare disease. It took me a few weeks just to be able to spell it! It was a blood disorder. They told me he wouldn't make it to his first birthday, but he did. He lived to be almost three years old."

I thought back to earlier that evening. I thought of Christian, my three-year-old, who came bounding onstage, full of life and mischief, intent on carrying out Barbara Johnson's suggestion to stick gum on my nose. I ducked, he laughed, and thousands of women laughed—but did she? Was the sight of my boy too painful a reminder of what she had been robbed of? She continued her story.

"As he got weaker and weaker I felt so helpless. There was nothing I could do. I began to pray; I began to read the Bible."

"Was your prayer that God would heal him?" I asked softly.

"That was part of it. Mostly, I just asked him to help us. When I finally handed my son to Christ, I handed all of me, too."

I had no words. For her, saying yes has left her with an open wound for the rest of her life. But she walks with it; she works with it. She is changed by it. I am aware again that there are those in my life who understand things I don't. Honestly, if losing your child is the price you pay for greater understanding, in all the honesty of my feeble humanity, I'd rather not gain it.

I think back to my experience in the hospital. I don't begin to compare a battle with clinical depression to the loss of a baby, but this mom's pain and grace reminded me of a conversation I had with a friend a year after I was released from the psychiatric unit.

"You are so different, Sheila," she said. "You seem so free."

"That's how I feel," I said. "It's as if God has given me a new life."

"I'm happy for you," she said. "But if that's the only way to get it, I'll pass!"

I smiled and hugged her. I knew exactly what she meant. I would not have chosen this path, but I cannot deny that walking it has changed me profoundly. There is something wonderful here, the edges of which I am still just scarcely scratching. There is a whole way of living that is so freeing, but I am still standing on the edge barely glimpsing it. I think I want to totally abandon myself to

God, to take that leap of faith, but I'm still standing. Perhaps you are too.

So why is it so hard for us to give an unreserved yes to God? I have a few guesses:

- We have a bruised picture of love.
- We operate out of fear rather than out of love.
- We feel we are victims of the whims of people and God alike.
- We are afraid God will treat us like trained animals jumping through hoops to entertain a bored deity.
- We don't know what we are saying yes to.

I'm sure you can come up with your own list of reasons why you are holding back. For me, the reasons feel deep and primal. My fear goes back further than I can recall—a weighty cold dread that tells me life is not safe. It warns that if I don't look after myself, who will? If I don't say no, someone—or worse still, God himself—will make me do something I don't want to do, all for the sake of the kingdom. And if it's for the kingdom, it would seem petty to refuse!

But saying no is suffocating me. I'm discovering the difference between living at peace and grasping control. I feel the difference between trust and fear. I live with a restless feeling that I'm settling for far less than what God wants for me.

It's like watching Christian with one of his gifts last Christmas. He held the box for the longest time, but he wouldn't open it because it was making a funny noise. Each time I picked it up and offered to open it for him he said, "No"— and made me put it down again. If I put it away in a closet, he made me bring it back out. Finally, when he wasn't looking, I took it into the kitchen and unwrapped the talking Barney he had asked for. He was over the moon when I gave it to him, but he wouldn't have risked opening the gift himself.

That's how I am. I skirt saying yes, but I don't want the package God is offering me out of my sight, because I have a feeling that what I've wanted all my life is in that very package.

MARY'S MEMORIES

JOY P. GAGE

from *The Treasures We Leave Behind*

Max Lucado posed twenty-five questions to Mary.

Songwriters Mark Lowry and Buddy Greene ask, "Mary, did you know that your baby boy would one day walk on water?"

I, in turn, would like to ask my own questions of her. These are burning questions that mothers everywhere would ask, such as, "At what point did the joy of a handmaiden turn to the sorrow of a mother?"

When you said, "I am the Lord's servant, may it be to me as you have said," did you have any idea that parental pain would be part of your lot?

When did you first know that your immortal son would die a mortal's death?

When the angel told you, "You are highly favored of God," did you know that your favored status would bring you to a rugged hill where your son would be crucified before your very eyes?

When you were told that the Lord would give Him the throne of His father David and that He would reign over the house of Judah forever, did you think that you would be mother of a God-King who would rule on earth in your lifetime?

When you learned that you, a virgin, and your old and barren cousin Elizabeth were both to give birth—when the angel told you that nothing is impossible with God—did you take that to mean that only good things could happen to these two sons of miraculous birth?

When Elizabeth said to you, "Blessed are you among women," did it occur to you that even blessed women experience sorrow if they are mothers?

When she said, "Blessed is she who has believed what the Lord has said to her will be accomplished," did you have any idea what God intended to accomplish?

When you sang, "My Spirit rejoices in God my Savior," did you know that the child you would bear would die in order to become your Savior?

When you sang, "From now on generations will call me blessed for the Mighty One has done great things for me," did you know there would be some "not so great things"?

When you laid your firstborn in the manger, did you know that He would become the "first born from the dead"?

On the eighth day when you named Him Jesus, did you remember that the angel had told Joseph that this child would save His people from their sins? Did you have any idea what that entailed?

When Simeon held your infant son and said, "My eyes have seen your salvation, a light for revelation to Gentiles and for glory to your people, Israel," why did you marvel at his words? What struck you most about his statement?

When he said to you, "And a sword will pierce your own soul too," did a chill clutch your heart?

Was that when you first knew that your son would suffer many things?

Is that when you first knew that your baby son, the Son of God, had come into the world only so that He could die for the world?

Did you think that you had let God down when you lost track of His Son for three days?

Why did you refer to Joseph as "your father" when you spoke to Jesus?

Did you feel rebuked when Jesus asked you, "Don't you know I must be about My Father's business?"

Did you know then that His Father's business would take Him to a wooden cross on Golgotha's hill?

Did you worry about Him when He was forty days out in the desert alone?

Were you frightened when the people from the synagogue in Nazareth drove Him out of town and took Him to the brow of the hill to throw Him over?

When He walked away unharmed, did you assume He was immortal?

Did you assume that no harm could ever come to Him?

When the Pharisees questioned His authority in the temple, did you want to defend your son as the Son of God?

When He raised a widow's son from the dead, did you think He would always exercise power over death?

Did He bring His disciples to your house?

Did you look at one of them with a mother's instinct and know that he was not good company for your son?

Did you feel a wrenching away when Jesus said He had no place to lay His head—when He rebuked a man who wanted to spend time with his family?

When you took your other sons and went to Capernaum to bring Jesus home, did you believe that you could convince Him to get more rest and take care of Himself?

When He refused to come, did you know that your motherly responsibilities had come to an end?

Was it hard to let go even though you knew this was the Son of God?

When He talked about division in families, did you feel you had already experienced it?

When did you first learn of His arrest?

Who went with you to the cross?

Were you comforted by His concern when He charged John with your care?

When He said, "I thirst," did you remember a small boy asking you for a drink?

Did you try to talk to Him on the cross?

Did you cringe when the soldiers pierced His side? Did you whisper a prayer of thanks that they didn't break His legs?

Did you see Him laid in the tomb?

Who walked home with you from Golgotha's hill?

Did you weep through the night?

Did you feel favored and blessed among women that night?

Were you at John's home when Mary Magdalene came running to tell him that the tomb was empty?

Did you know then that the Savior of the world had crossed the chasm between mortality and immortality?

Did you see Him in His resurrection body?

When did you know that death had been swallowed up in victory?

When did the sorrow of a mother turn to the joy of a handmaid?

Did you save some treasured keepsake from His days as a carpenter, or were you content with a mother's memories and a believer's hope?

This story of Mary's memories is taken from Luke 1:26–56; 2; 4; John 19:28; 20:18; Mark 3:21, 31–34.

IS THIS A ROAD TEST?

CHONDA PIERCE

from *Chonda Pierce On Her Soapbox*

The only way to explain the boxes of old baby clothes in my attic is to say that the day after Chera came home from the hospital, she grew up. Just like that. How could fifteen years have gone by so quickly? Yesterday I was rocking her to sleep—and today? Today I'm biting every fingernail on my right hand. (The left hand went during labor.) Because, at fifteen years of age, as every mother of teenagers or preteens knows, your baby obtains a driver's permit. (My prayer request should be obvious by now.)

Chera was only a few days past fifteen when we drove to the exam station. The room was full of parents (who looked older than I) and little children. But, as we waited our turn (for almost an hour!), I realized these little children, who were fifteen- and sixteen-year-olds, were coming together for one purpose and one purpose only: to make it legal for them to slip behind the wheel of their parents' car. (Whatever happened to the legislation that would move the driving age to, say, thirty-five—but, only after the child had purchased said vehicle herself?)

Chera filled out the application and held it in one hand. In the other, she held a battered, rolled-up copy of the driver's manual she had been studying for the last several months. She was taking these last few minutes to study the shapes of signs and the various distances any driver is supposed to maintain when he or she is following someone, or there's a train crossing the street, or if it's wet or dry. As we waited, she was proud to rattle off all these numbers, measurements, colors, and shapes. For just a moment there, I was reminded of her earlier years, watching *Sesame Street* and getting so excited when she learned to tell a square from a triangle or the color blue from yellow.

The routine in this busy place quickly became apparent. First, we waited until our number was called. When it was our turn, we handed in the application. While Chera took a quick eye exam, I signed a piece of paper that stated I would be financially responsible for any damage Chera might do out on our public highways, at least until she was eighteen. Chera passed her vision test, and I added a little note to my sheet that this financial obligation would probably go on a lot longer than that.

I soon noticed that the other parents were experiencing varying degrees of uneasiness. Chera was there only to get a permit—just to take a test and that's it. But other kids were there for the real thing: a license. Their training was over. The parents of these kids seemed more anxious, more frightened, more sickly (you get the picture).

All the chairs were taken, so most of us stood in little clusters until every so often someone from the other side of the counter would call out a name. "Redmond! Testing station #4 is open." And a kid (I'm guessing a kid with the last name of Redmond) stepped out from the crowd and into an adjoining room where one long wall was lined with computer terminals. The Redmond kid turned and gave a thumbs-up. Someone who looked just like him (only older) returned the thumbs-up. "Johnson! Testing station #7 is open." Off went another future driver. She stopped long enough to smile and wave back at her mother. Her mother sort of giggled.

"Wilson!" came the voice from the other side of the counter again. "ROAD TEST!" This is when things changed. I saw Wilson step out from the crowd, and the parent of that child put a hand up to her mouth and gasp, as if she had just leaped into a pool of ice water. I could only watch, feeling a small portion of her pain, her anguish, her financial obligation, as she was put to the test. Her child, a young man with a fuzzy mustache (I *think* it was a mustache) sort of loped away the way only gangly teenagers can do, thumbs in his belt loops, shoulders bent over. He glanced back over his shoulder and forced a grin at his mom, as if to say, "Gee, Mom, cool it. Everything's rad, so take a chill pill. It's just a road test." But I could tell, as a parent, that would be a hard pill to take. I looked at Chera, but she hadn't noticed anything; she was trying to recall the maximum jail time for first- and second-time DUI convictions.

Chera was sent to testing station #2. I stood in the corral with the rest of the parents and watched her push different spots on the computer screen as she answered the questions, trying to imagine her behind the wheel of the family van. She was supposed to answer thirty questions, missing no more than six—but after twenty-four, the machine stopped and dismissed her. She stood up and walked out to me, a bit stiff from nerves, and said, "I think I got them all right."

"All of them?" I said (but I shouldn't have been surprised). "You mean, it didn't beep or buzz or anything like that?"

She shook her head. "No. Actually, it was quite easy. And most of them were common sense, like, if you cross the street at night you should (a) wear light-colored clothes; (b) wait until the sun comes up; or (c) cross in front of big trucks."

I wondered if people who missed this question ever drove through my neighborhood.

As Chera realized that one tough part was over and she wouldn't have to carry that old, battered driving manual around anymore, she also figured out that the toughest part was yet to come: the picture. She combed her hair and practiced smiling. "How does this look?" she asked, flashing a perfect smile. "Tilt your head a bit this way," I said, feeling I had to give her some instruction or she wouldn't believe me.

Even though she looked beautiful, and even though the testing instructor had to show her perfect score off to everyone there at the counter, Chera took one look at her driver's permit photo and said, "It makes my head look squished."

I just smiled and said, "They only get worse."

I let her drive on the straight road home. We hadn't gone very far when we approached a van going in the other direction with its turn signal on. Chera came to a quick and complete stop, almost standing on the brakes.

"What are you doing?" I asked. The thought of that form I'd signed earlier flashed through my mind.

Just then another car pulled up from a side street. Chera rose from her seat a little so she could mash the brakes down even farther. Both the people in the van and the car stared at us.

I stared at Chera. "I'm yielding! I'm yielding!" she shouted, her knuckles white around the steering wheel.

"But, Chera, you have the right of way," I said, trying not to get too excited so she wouldn't get too excited. After a few moments of this, the guy in the van threw his hands up in frustration, not sure what to do.

"The book says never assume you have the right of way!" Chera said.

The guy in the car waved a thank-you—as if we were being polite—and shot out in front of us. Finally the guy in the van got tired of Chera's "yield" and turned in front of us.

"But you can't yield when everyone else is yielding to you," I explained.

Chera looked at me with a determined expression. "I can out-yield anyone!" And then she added, "As long as I'm two car lengths away. Now, do I turn here or go straight?"

I imagined my expression must have been the same as the woman's back at the testing station whose son loped off to take a road test. Here was my baby girl, the one who had gotten car sick and thrown up as [a] little child on the backseat of this very van, the one who had left crayons to melt in the sun on the backseat of this very van, the same one who had eaten dozens of Happy Meals on the backseat of this very van. And now she was behind the wheel, mashing the gas, standing on the brake, and yielding on busy highways.

A year from now, I thought, *we'll probably be back in that same testing station, and someone from the other side of the counter will call "Pierce, ROAD TEST!" and Chera will lope off to show what she can do on the highway (maybe even parallel park) while I twist my face into expressions that will alarm other parents watching me.*

So I am determined that we will practice every day. She will become comfortable with the gas, the brakes, the turn signals, the seat belts, the wipers. She will know when to slow down and when to accelerate, how to merge and how *not* to merge. And most important, I will teach her when to yield and when *not* to yield. She will be able, when the day of the road test comes, to pass the test.

But then again, since the day she was born, we've been preparing her for her real ROAD TEST. And that test, one long and seemingly endless test, has nothing to do with cars.

HANDS OFF THE HANDIWORK!

PATTY STUMP

As the pottery class ended, Elisabeth enthusiastically bounded in my direction with a glowing report regarding her most recent artistic accomplishments: "Mom, you'll never believe what we made today. I can't wait to show you!" In the course of the week-long class, she had enjoyed opportunities to form and fashion a variety of clay pieces that remained carefully out of sight until the Friday finale—the ultimate unveiling of her carefully crafted keepsakes.

Anxiously, I waited to see what my daughter had created, and each day when I picked her up I sought to *sneak a peek* at the mounds of clay creations. As the week neared its end, Elisabeth invited me in to see her handiwork. Enthusiastically, she directed my eyes toward a handful of pottery pieces she had sought to skillfully sculpt. As we made our way around the room, she led me to her final work of art and eagerly asked me what I thought. Studying the mound of clay, I struggled to identify just what the figure was meant to be.

"It looks just like one, doesn't it?" she asked.

Muttering a few unintelligible remarks, I finally told her that it was the cutest duck I'd ever seen.

"It's not a duck, it's a dog!" she replied. "It's going into the kiln tonight, and tomorrow we can pick it up. The teacher said it will look *even better* after it's been fired."

Hmmm . . . even better?

Encouraging Elisabeth to join her grandmother, who was waiting outside, I pondered my daughter's delight regarding her prized pup. Hoping to heighten her joy, I picked up the clay canine and subtly made a couple of minor modifications: a simple poke to more clearly define his ears, along with a tiny touch to his stubby tail. There! I was confident my daughter would be thrilled with her work and how the kiln had slightly refined its features.

The next afternoon my daughter emerged from her much-anticipated class in tears. As she choked back her emotions, Elisabeth stated that something had happened to her dog while in the kiln. Assuming her puppy lay in pieces, I hurried inside to assess the mess. Much to my surprise, I was delighted to discover sitting on the table before me an adorable little brown dog.

Seeking to reassure Elisabeth that her puppy was in one piece, she glanced at the figure and shared a surprising perspective. Elisabeth said that she knew her piece didn't look much like a dog before it went into the kiln, but that it had looked just the way she wanted it to. Now, much to her disappointment, her carefully crafted piece bore little or no resemblance to the prior work.

The Lord taught me an unexpected lesson that day: at the heart of a creator is a unique vision for each piece they form and fashion. While the outcome may appear to be less than best, in the eyes of the creator their handiwork bears beauty and worth beyond measure. So it is with God's creation of each of us. As a mom, I continue to discover the beauty of what God has created within each of my children. I've come to recognize that often those areas or attributes that I identify as needing slight adjustments may actually be qualities that I simply need to view from a different perspective. I continue to learn as well that sometimes keeping our hands off the handiwork is best.

Psalm 139:14 states that we are fearfully and wonderfully made—creatively crafted by God and beautiful to behold.

STOLEN FLOWERS

LOIS PECCE

Rwanda, Africa: New Year's Day 1949. I watched with growing indignation as one national after another mounted the steps to the back porch and offered my mother a fistful of lantana blossoms. "New Year's greetings, Madame."

Mom stood at a small table cutting long, pungent bars of naphtha soap into one-and-a-half-inch slices, handing a piece to each well-wisher who came. "Thank you," she'd reply. "A happy New Year to you also. Here is our gift for you."

"But, Mom," I said heatedly during a break in the line, "those flowers are from your garden; from your own hedge. The Africans are stealing your flowers and you're accepting them like a gift."

"The flowers don't belong to us," she replied. "They belong to the land—to everyone. We just help them grow. Besides, these are proud people. Soap is precious to them and they feel better about accepting it if they can give us something too. Here," she handed me the latest bunches of rose, yellow, and orange blossoms, "please put these in some water."

I took the flowers and went indoors, still not convinced by my mother's logic. Sounds of chatter drew me to the window. Sure enough, another group of Africans was stripping handfuls of blossoms from the hedge, laughing and talking as they went around to the kitchen door to greet my mother and receive their soap. I didn't understand their words but I felt sure they were mocking her. I scowled. If Mom only knew how she was being laughed at!

This was my first awareness of the practice of exchanging gifts on New Year's Day rather than at Christmas. Mom explained that the New Year's tradition of gift exchange likely began during the days of Belgium colonialism in Rwanda. To me, it seemed strange. Getting soap for a gift seemed strange too, though I understood a little about the need. Soap was not affordable or accessible to the general populace. The grainy yellow bars that came in wooden crates to the mission hospital were the all-purpose soap for surgery prep, laundry, dishes, shampoo, and baths. We learned early not to waste soap or water. (Water was carried in large clay pots, borne on the heads of Africans, from a spring two miles away. Mother taught us that each drop was precious.)

Still I fretted about the flowers. For much of my barely nine years, most spent in this very house, Mom suffered repeated battles with me about unauthorized flower collecting. The beauty and variety of the tropical blooms growing in our yard overlooking Lake Kivu enchanted me. I'd walk through the gardens first thing in the morning to discover what new beauty awaited. The more I looked and admired, the more covetous I became until, too often, the forbidden treasures lay bruised and wilting in my hands. I'd quickly hide the evidence of my disobedience, but somehow Mother always knew. Now here were these Africans picking flowers without permission and she was smiling and saying "Thanks." Jealousy and anger ate deep into my heart.

Years later, after Mom's death, I recalled the incident with new understanding. As a young couple newly graduated from college, my parents committed themselves to overseas medical ministry. Dad, a physician, took specialized training in tropical diseases. Their assignment was a remote station in the mountains of Rwanda. After a long, harrowing journey, they reached the end of a narrow, winding dirt road. From that point near the top of a mountain they looked toward their destination, twelve miles away, accessible only by foot. Agile, surefooted porters balanced my parents' few possessions atop their heads. Another four carried a large woven gondola on their shoulders bearing Mom, my sister (aged two), and me (aged three months). Dad walked.

In this place of beauty and deadly unseen enemies (malaria, yellow fever, black-water fever, leprosy, yaws) they established their lives. A year later they buried their first son, stillborn after Mother fell on the stone steps to the vegetable garden during her eighth month of pregnancy. Communication with the outside world, which at that time was in the throes of World War II, was slow and limited. African runners carried mail or messages across the hills and mountains. Supplies for home and hospital were brought by dugout canoe from the nearest town ninety-five miles away. Letters and parcels from America took up to six months to arrive.

In this circumstance, so different from anything she had known, Mom dedicated herself to service. It formed the basis of her life. In all her years I never heard Mother sigh for things she couldn't have, complain about hardship, or grumble about hard work. Her attitude about the Africans and the flowers symbolized, to me, her attitude about serving Christ. He came to give us what we needed most. He also knew that we needed to give something back in order to enter relationship with him and appreciate his gift, even though whatever we gave was already his in the first place.

I finally realized that the conflict with my mother over picking flowers was never really about flowers. It was about a deep-rooted selfishness and greed in my soul. She wanted me to know the freedom of owning nothing, coveting nothing. She wanted me to understand that everything belongs to God and that happiness is not in holding on to things but in holding onto him and enjoying what he provides.

SECTION Eight

The PROVISION
OF A MOTHER

RED BALLOON

HOLLY DAVIS

My daughter, Cassie, sat in her car booster seat clutching the string of a red balloon—or not clutching it. Knowing her prize would float no higher than the car ceiling, she'd pull it down and let it float, pull it down and let it float. Mastery. The world spun just for her. Hadn't she just come from the carnival with Mommy? Hadn't the last several hours revolved around her entertainment? The red balloon was her scepter.

We pulled into the driveway and got out of the car. A short walk to the front door and we'd be back to the haven where all good adventures end.

But I hadn't even unlocked the front door when I heard Cassie's cry. The balloon had escaped! She'd released it to push back her hair, sure she'd be able to grab the string again. Hadn't she done it a thousand times in the car? How could the balloon have risen so quickly?

And I, her mother, protector, provider of fun times, restorer of lost things, even I'd failed to grab the string in time to save the balloon. "Oh, honey, I'm sorry, but your balloon's gone. See? It's free!"

Cassie didn't care about setting the balloon free. She wanted the balloon to come indoors and play with her. All the fun of the day was fading to nothing with the disappearing balloon, which was floating across the street toward the neighbor's tree. Would it clear the branches? No! It caught. Yet it was still gone, like an escaped parrot that chooses the lure of the wild over its owner's friendship.

"I can't reach it, honey, but you can see it from your bedroom window. It's an outdoor balloon."

Cassie wailed. Life had betrayed her. What good were carnivals if they ended in lost balloons? I would have hugged her, but she wriggled away. What good were hugs when a balloon was lost?

Having my hug rejected tore me in ways unfathomable to Cassie. She'd have to become a mother before she'd have an inkling of that pain, and motherhood for Cassie was, at best, years away. So I bore the pain alone—not just the pain of seeing my child's distress over the lost balloon, but of seeing my child turn from my comfort.

Cassie couldn't understand my feelings, but I could understand hers. I was the provider of red balloons, but I hadn't made the balloon stay. I was the guide and financier of carnival visits, but I didn't guarantee the visit would end happily. All she could see was loss.

"Cassie," I reasoned, "you had a wonderful time at the carnival. The balloon was just a small part. Be happy for what you have and let the balloon go."

Cassie cried.

I hurried her into the house to divert her attention. She raced to her upstairs bedroom to look at the balloon from the window.

Then I heard her shriek.

"Mommy!"

I flew to Cassie's room where she pointed to the tree, unable to speak in her anxiety. The balloon string had loosened from its branch. We held our breath as the balloon floated higher—then sighed in relief when the string caught again. Cassie was learning appreciation. Even a balloon in a tree was better than a balloon lost forever.

That's when I remembered that we had a tree-trimming pole—a telescoped contraption with a saw-toothed blade on the end, used to cut tree branches. Had I waited too long? Was the balloon too high? Why did the balloon have to be so important?

"Let me try something, honey."

I wasn't sure my idea would work, so I didn't explain my plan, I just made a beeline for the garage to retrieve the pole. Cassie quickly caught on. Hope widened her eyes. Silence replaced her cries.

With the pole as our banner, we dashed across the street. The jagged blade was perfect for catching the string, but what if the blade scraped the balloon?

Cassie, seeing the danger, whimpered.

Oh, Lord, I prayed, *don't let me burst the balloon!*

The Lord answered my prayer. The string caught and the balloon came down. Halfway back to the house, Cassie stopped, overcome by an impulse to give me a hug. I was the heroine, restorer of lost red balloons, the all-wise, all-sufficient mom. I liked this new role, trivial as the service was that had brought it about. I'd have done much, much more to make Cassie smile.

In fact, I did do much, much more daily, not just to make Cassie smile, but to make her life good in every way. I cooked her meals, washed her clothes, read her stories, worked to help support the family, raced home to spend time with the family, stayed up late, rose to rescue her from night fears, got up early, indulged, disciplined. I did so many more things of so much greater significance than retrieving red balloons, but seldom did I receive the heroine's hug for those other things. They were too ordinary.

I think this is the way we all behave toward our heavenly Father. Daily he provides us with blessings innumerable—color, sound, speech, family, friends, food, laughter, sun, and stars. The list fills the universe. Even greater than those blessings is salvation, the promise not only of life eternal, but of a much better life.

We give him thanks, but perhaps we amuse him with the emphasis we give to certain blessings over others. Perhaps we draw on his patience when we fret over some "red balloon," forgetting all we have.

I imagine him reasoning with me: "Why are you troubled over one red balloon? I can restore that balloon. If I choose not to restore it, I will still restore you. Trust me, child. I love you in ways you cannot fathom."

If only we'd grasp the concept of God's provision instead of grasping at red balloons. Then we'd see that all the lost, deflated, and burst red balloons of this present time are not worthy to be compared with the blessings we have and the glories to be revealed.

ON SALE AT YOUR LOCAL CHRISTIAN BOOKSTORE

CHONDA PIERCE

from *Second Row, Piano Side*

I t was an exciting month. I had finally completed my first full-length comedy video and for weeks had been awaiting the news of its release. Earlier, David and I had sat across a big conference table with Mary Kraker and Norman Holland at Chapel Music Group and negotiated a recording lease and distribution agreement with them. I had tried to be so professional, but deep down inside I was jumping up and down like a little girl. Soon my videos, compact discs, and cassettes would be in hundreds of Christian bookstores across the country!

I couldn't believe it! For years, I must admit, I've had this secret fantasy to be hanging out in a bookstore—perhaps looking for the latest Max Lucado book—when I'm approached by a stranger who studies first my face and then the cover of my latest video and says, "Hey—isn't this you?"

Finally the release date came. I knew they were out there. It was time to check them out. (Besides, the next Max Lucado book was out too. No harm in jetting down to the local bookstore!) I quickly discovered that I didn't make the front window, nor the rack by the cash register. I didn't even make the bargain bin! Exasperated, I finally asked the sales clerk, "Where am I?" She promptly led me to a section filled with books about psychology and left me alone.

A few days later I tried again, then again and again. Nothing. (Although I did catch up on all the Max Lucado books I was missing.) Finally, while I had several days to be home, I called my local bookstore and asked if they could check their computer to see if the project really existed. The young clerk said, "Yes, ma'am. And every time we get a few of them in, we sell them all out the same day. We have some now, but you'd better hurry. They're going quick." I couldn't believe it. Complete strangers were going into their local Christian bookstore to purchase a comedy tape of me—and not Mark Lowry!

I was so excited. My mother is going to be so proud of me, I thought. I decided to hop into my car and pick her up and take her to the bookstore and surprise her, maybe we'd even spot someone making a buy. When I got to Mom's, she was putting on her coat and scarf and was in a hurry to leave. "Oh, hi, Honey!" she greeted me. "I was just going to the mall. Want to go?" On her dining room table were about 14 Chonda Pierce videos. I asked her where she had gotten them and what she was doing with them. She said, "Honey, I've been going to the bookstore every few days and buying these for Christmas presents. The nice young man from the bookstore just called and said some more have just come in. Your Uncle Gerald will love one of these! And Cousin Brad and Nancy—come on. We have to hurry!" She ushered me out the door.

"Going fast," the man had said. "I'll sure be glad when they put them in the bargain bin, won't you?"

On the way to the mall she asked me what I was doing with all those Max Lucado books in the backseat.

"Christmas presents," I mumbled.

A SATISFIED THIRST

MAX LUCADO

from *The Applause of Heaven*

Mommy I'm so thirsty. I want a drink."

Susanna Petroysan heard her daughter's pleas, but there was nothing she could do. She and four-year-old Gayaney were trapped beneath tons of collapsed concrete and steel. Beside them in the darkness lay the body of Susanna's sister-in-law, Karine, one of the fifty-five thousand victims of the worst earthquake in the history of Soviet Armenia.

Calamity never knocks before it enters, and this time, it had torn down the door.

Susanna had gone to Karine's house to try on a dress. It was December 7, 1988, at 11:30 A.M. The quake hit at 11:41. She had just removed the dress and was clad in stockings and a slip when the fifth-floor apartment began to shake. Susanna grabbed her daughter but had taken only a few steps before the floor opened up and they tumbled in. Susanna, Gayaney, and Karine fell into the basement with the nine-story apartment house crumbling around them.

"Mommy, I need a drink. Please give me something."

There was nothing for Susanna to give.

She was trapped flat on her back. A concrete panel eighteen inches above her head and a crumpled water pipe above her shoulders kept her from standing. Feeling around in the darkness, she found a twenty-four-ounce jar of blackberry jam that had fallen into the basement. She gave the entire jar to her daughter to eat. It was gone by the second day.

"Mommy, I'm so thirsty."

Susanna knew she would die, but she wanted her daughter to live. She found a dress, perhaps the one she had come to try on, and made a bed for Gayaney. Though it was bitter cold, she took off her stockings and wrapped them around the child to keep her warm.

The two were trapped for eight days.

Because of the darkness, Susanna lost track of time. Because of the cold, she lost the feeling in her fingers and toes. Because of her inability to move, she lost hope. "I was just waiting for death."

She began to hallucinate. Her thoughts wandered. A merciful sleep occasionally freed her from the horror of her entombment, but the sleep would be brief. Something always awakened her: the cold, the hunger, or—most often—the voice of her daughter.

"Mommy, I'm thirsty."

At some point in that eternal night, Susanna had an idea. She remembered a television program about an explorer in the Arctic who was dying of thirst. His comrade slashed open his hand and gave his friend his blood.

"I had no water, no fruit juice, no liquids. It was then I remembered I had my own blood."

Her groping fingers, numb from the cold, found a piece of shattered glass. She sliced open her left index finger and gave it to her daughter to suck.

The drops of blood weren't enough. "Please, Mommy, some more. Cut another finger." Susanna has no idea how many times she cut herself. She only knows that if she hadn't, Gayaney would have died. Her blood was her daughter's only hope.

———

"This cup is the new covenant in my blood," Jesus explained, holding up the wine. Luke 22:20 (NIV)

The claim must have puzzled the apostles. They had been taught the story of the Passover wine. It symbolized the lamb's blood that the Israelites, enslaved long ago in Egypt, had painted on the doorposts of their homes. That blood had kept death from their homes and saved their firstborn. It had helped deliver them from the clutches of the Egyptians.

For thousands of generations the Jews had observed the Passover by sacrificing the lambs. Every year the blood would be poured, and every year the deliverance would be celebrated.

The law called for spilling the blood of a lamb. That would be enough.

It would be enough to fulfill the law. It would be enough to satisfy the command. It would be enough to justify God's justice.

But it would not be enough to take away sin.

" . . . because it is impossible for the blood of bulls and goats to take away sins." Hebrews 10:4 (NIV)

Sacrifices could offer temporary solutions, but only God could offer the eternal one.

So he did.

Beneath the rubble of a fallen world, he pierced his hands. In the wreckage of a collapsed humanity, he ripped open his side. His children were trapped, so he gave his blood.

It was all he had. His friends were gone. His strength was waning. His possessions had been gambled away at his feet. Even his Father had turned his head. His blood was all he had. But his blood was all it took.

"If anyone is thirsty," Jesus once said, "let him come to me and drink." (John 7:37 NIV)

Admission of thirst doesn't come easy for us. False fountains pacify our cravings with sugary swallows of pleasure. But there comes a time when pleasure doesn't satisfy. There comes a dark hour in every life when the world caves in and we are left trapped in the rubble of reality, parched and dying.

Some would rather die than admit it. Others admit it and escape death.

"God, I need help."

So the thirsty come. A ragged lot we are, bound together by broken dreams and collapsed promises. Fortunes that were never made. Families that were never built. Promises that were never kept. Wide-eyed children trapped in the basement of our own failures.

And we are very thirsty.

Not thirsty for fame, possessions, passion, or romance. We've drunk from those pools. They are salt water in the desert. They don't quench—they kill.

"Blessed are those who hunger and thirst for righteousness. . . ."

Righteousness. That's it. That's what we are thirsty for. We're thirsty for a clean conscience. We crave a clean slate. We yearn for a fresh start. We pray for a hand which will enter the dark cavern of our world and do for us the one thing we can't do for ourselves—make us right again.

———

"Mommy, I'm so thirsty," Gayaney begged.

"It was then I remembered I had my own blood," Susanna explained.

And the hand was cut, and the blood was poured, and the child was saved.

"God, I'm so thirsty," we pray.

"It is my blood, the blood of the new agreement," Jesus stated, "shed to set many free from their sins." (Matthew 26:28 PHILLIPS)

And the hand was pierced,
> and the blood was poured,
>> and the children are saved.

SIPPY CUP TRUST

TAMARA RICE

Peering down the stairs with dread, I tightened my grip on the overflowing diaper bag and clutched baby Maddie to my side. "Nicholas, hold onto the rail," I said to my three-year-old with what I must admit was more irritation than concern.

"But, Mom," he protested, holding up his favorite spill-proof cup with both hands, "I got my juicy!" (Implying, of course, that with two hands on the yellow-and-blue cup, he couldn't be expected to grasp the railing!)

"You only need one hand for your sippy cup, Nick. Now hold onto the rail."

I teetered down the outside stairs of our apartment behind Nick and his cup, praying for what had to be the millionth time that I wouldn't trip or lose my balance and injure one of my children on the concrete steps.

How I hated that staircase! Each trip down those stairs (not to mention up) was a painful reminder that our plans to buy a home had recently been postponed—halted, if not thwarted altogether. My husband's long awaited raise had not been granted. This meant we would be spending at least another year in the small upstairs apartment we'd been calling home since before Nick was born.

I knew God was watching over us. He had always provided for our needs. But I felt like he hadn't been paying much attention lately. Didn't he know our family had outgrown the apartment? Didn't he see how badly our energetic little son needed a yard? Had God been taking a lunch break the last time I struggled up those stairs with two gallons of milk, a baby, and an unruly preschooler in tow?

I wasn't *mad* at God. Just hurt. And frustrated.

It was going to be one of *those* days again, I realized, as our groaning garage door revealed the disheartening sight of my beat-up old car and all our belongings that wouldn't fit upstairs—one of those days where I had to fight the feelings of disappointment and frustration all day long.

I was heading to Bible study where—appropriately enough—we were studying Philippians: the book of joy. The same book where Paul wrote those famous words about being content, whatever the circumstance. *Ha!* I thought, securing Maddie into her car seat and tossing the diaper bag onto the floorboard. *Paul never lived in an upstairs apartment with two small children.*

"Mom, look at that!" Nick brought me out from my cloud of self-pity momentarily, pointing excitedly to a spider on the wall of the garage. "*Wow!*"

"Wow," I echoed weakly, opening the door on his side. "We're gonna be late, so get in the car, buddy."

He obeyed quickly (for once) and attempted to climb up into his car seat while still clutching his sippy cup. He resisted my assistance, straining and pulling upward with his free hand until his patience gave out and the beloved cup crashed loudly onto the concrete as the sudden, desperate strength of both his arms catapulted him into his seat. "Mom!" He turned back, eyes wide with horror and hands stretched frantically toward the ground, where his cup of juice was now rolling lazily toward the front tire. "Mom, get it! I dropped my juicy!"

"Just a second, Nick. Let's get you buckled in first."

As an experienced mother, I knew if I bent over to pick up the cup first, he'd just bolt out of his car seat and into the front of the car and we'd be ten minutes late to Bible study instead of five. "First things first," I said knowingly.

But the loss of his precious sippy cup evoked total panic in Nick. "My juicy! My juicy! Get it, Mom! Please! Get it!"

If I had a dollar for every time I'd heard the crash of that same cup on the ground and those familiar, insistent cries to get it, we certainly wouldn't still be living in that apartment.

I held him down with one hand while wrestling the worn car seat straps over his flailing body with the other. "I see your sippy cup," I said as calmly as I could, "and I'll pick it up after you're strapped in."

We'd been through this routine so many times it seemed as if I were stuck in some reoccurring bad dream as his stressed-out cries continued. "But, Mom! My juicy! I need it! I need it!"

"I see your sippy cup," I repeated, seizing the ounce of patience that nearly eluded me, "And I promise you I won't forget it. We won't leave without it."

His panic escalated, as it always did. Nevertheless, I struggled to secure him into the car seat, which I knew was more important than retrieving the cup. Then, suddenly, with one glorious click of the seat belt, it was done—he was buckled in. I bent down, grabbed the yellow-and-blue cup from the ground, and pressed it into his eager hands. "You see?" I couldn't resist saying, "I told you I wouldn't forget your juicy!"

I slid behind the wheel, reveling in amazement that no matter how many times I had retrieved that cup for Nick in the past, he still didn't trust me to remember it. *Doesn't he know I always see it fall? Doesn't he hear me when I say I won't forget it, and we won't leave without it? Why can't he just trust that I'm in control, sit still, and let me handle things?*

I wish I could say I recognized the irony instantly, but I confess it wasn't until about an hour later, while sitting at the Bible study, that it hit me.

For weeks I'd been wrestling with God over our apartment. Questioning him, not convinced that he understood our needs. But it was only that morning after the umpteenth sippy cup incident that I realized God had been with me all along, watching me, doing what was best for me, and wanting me to settle down and trust him. I was flailing around in my heart, crying out, and complaining, "Don't you see what's happening, God? Fix it! Fix it!" All the while he'd been shaking his head, saying, "Do you think I don't see? Did you think I would forget? Have I ever once forgotten?"

I realized then that the most patient and caring Parent in the universe knows my needs before I ask. He has met them before, is meeting them now, and will meet them again. All I have to do is sit patiently and quietly while he takes care of things.

OPERATION ENDURING SLEEP

DENA J. DYER

We call it Operation Enduring Sleep. My husband and I, the two-member coalition in this war on sleep deprivation, take our assignment very seriously. The mission: to transfer our sleeping toddler, Jordan, from his car seat to his bed without waking him.

After we deploy ourselves, our first step is to release the buckle on our son's restraining device. Jordan sighs, and we freeze. Our lips purse, our foreheads crease, and we both wonder if we'll make it.

After unlatching our little soldier, we give silent instructions to one another. Carey mouths, "You get him, I'll get the door." I nod in agreement.

Holding my breath, I slip Jordan's car seat strap over his head. So far, so good. Now the risky part: the hoist. I carefully bring my son's arms up over my shoulders, wrap my arm around his waist, and cover his head—so as not to bump it on the car door and accidentally end the operation.

My husband holds the door for me, and I walk gently past him. Trooper that he is, Carey has already been on a stealth mission in our son's bedroom. We both know that any miscalculation or stumble on my part would prove fatal to our plan, so my hubby has pulled the bedcovers back, darkened the room, and conducted a ground search for stray objects on the floor.

As I reach the target, Jordan stirs a bit. I hesitate, recalculate, and start humming a lullaby. Carey follows stealthily behind me, whispering encouragement. "Almost there," he says.

Then ever so gently, I place Jordan on his bed, take off his shoes, and cover him with a blanket. I tiptoe away, giving Carey the thumbs-up sign. Mission accomplished.

As we struggle to keep from waking our son, it occurs to me that God does the same for me. When I'm worried or fearful, God says, "Peace, be still." He comforts my heart so I can rest in him. But all too often I rebel and try to handle things on my own. I don't want to rest in his will—I want to be awake and active. (Even when I need the rest!)

"Mommy," I hear. Carey groans quietly. My heart starts to race. *No,* I think. *We've come too far to fail now! I need a nap, too.* I decide to walk away slowly, ignore my child, and hope he's not really awake.

"Mommy!" Jordan cries, louder this time. I grimace at Carey. He shrugs, and I turn back to our child's room. Our son is sitting up in bed, rubbing his eyes. "I'm not tired now."

"You need more rest," I whisper. "Go back to sleep."

Jordan hops off his bed, runs to my side, and raises his arms. "I want to hold you!" he says.

And so the mission is aborted. *Sneaky kid,* I think. He knows my weak spots, and he isn't afraid to exploit them.

Thankfully, God never fails to hold me when I need him. And although I have weak spots, he doesn't. He's quick to forgive, quick to love, and slow to anger. Someday I hope I'll be half the parent to my child that God is to me.

THE BIRTHDAY SURPRISE

DIANE H. PITTS

The year was 1961. The air was electrified with the crispness of fall, and excitement whirled about me. As I skipped to Edgewood School, I was sure everyone could see that today I was eight years old. My red-checkered dress rustled in the breeze and a shiny gold locket reflected the morning sun.

I thought back over the summer, when I had hinted several times for one of two birthday surprises—a horse, or a watch. My friend Deborah who lived across the dirt road in our little southern town had a beautiful Tennessee Walker. She allowed me to ride him anytime, but I wanted my own horse.

I clutched my books tightly as I neared the school and imagined owning a horse instead of borrowing Deborah's. My birthday horse didn't need to be a thoroughbred; a pony would do.

Just then a thought struck like a boulder. What if I didn't get a horse? Hope began to disintegrate with the impact. My chest felt heavy and my throat constricted. Well, I gulped, there was always the watch. Maybe that would be all right. I quickened my steps and smiled slowly. My best friend and I would giggle and compare our watches at recess. Mine would be gold to match my locket, and oh, how it would shine! Thoughts about the watch scattered like the sun's rays as I saw children flooding into the school doors and realized I might be late. Just another good reason I needed that watch!

All through the day I watched the clock creep toward 2:30. I whispered to the air, "Soon." With the first vibrations of the dismissal bell, I was hurtling out the door like a horse from the starting gate. I raced to our brown Ford and climbed in the back, but quickly reined in my giddiness.

"Hi, Mama," I said breathlessly as I laid my books on the seat beside me and waited.

My mother was generally quiet and reserved, but she loved giving surprises.

Easter, Christmas, and birthdays were always special at our house, and I could sense that today would be no different. She turned and looked over her shoulder and replied with a small grin.

"How is the birthday girl? Wonder what birthday surprise is waiting?"

I propped my arms over the front seat and looked out the window. "Very soon," I murmured. We drove slowly through town. Would we stop on the outskirts at a farm, or would we go to Hick's Jewelers? I was so busy daydreaming I hardly noticed when we bumped into the curb that skirted an unfamiliar house.

"Well, here we are," my mother said softly.

I didn't see a farm, and this didn't look like a jewelry store. *Maybe she already has the watch,* I reasoned and searched for the concealed package. I grabbed faintly at the hope that I was missing something. My mother must have seen the confusion on my face because she brightened and explained, "Your daddy and I wanted to give you something very special. This is your first day of piano lessons." She looked at me expectantly. "We even found an upright piano that's being delivered today."

I fought the urge to cry. Swallowing disappointment, I smiled back. I hadn't considered music. Maybe it wouldn't be so bad; it was just unexpected.

"That's great, Mama. It sure is a surprise."

She got out of the old car first. I followed her up the stairs, away from a horse and a watch and toward a significant door in my life. *Oh, Mama,* I thought dejectedly, *how could you?*

We walked into a chilly room warmed by a space heater, and I sat down on the creaking piano bench. Over the next thirty minutes, Mrs. Adams, the piano teacher, introduced me to the world of music. Unhurriedly, she drew me in with the melodies, and the chill in my spirit melted away. My mother had chosen a gift that unlocked my soul.

Forty years later, I marvel at my mother's wise decision and financial sacrifice in giving me those piano lessons. Numerous doors opened over the decades. When I was too shy to speak, music spoke for me. I traveled to Europe to perform in an international choral festival. I served as a church musician for over thirty years, and even taught piano when I needed money to attend school.

Music has allowed me to make friends easily, and serve God as well.

Today there are moments I find myself questioning God or the things he allows, and I lash out, *"God, how could you?"* Then I recall another place in time, a mother's heart I did not understand, and a birthday surprise I almost failed to accept. Similarly, the mother-heart of God makes wise decisions when he leads me away from unnecessary things and through doors I don't always understand—long years of singleness, a debilitating illness, and even the death of a child. On numerous occasions I have been blind to the benefits of his choices, yet he makes them. Trusting his wisdom has not been easy, but it has been right.

My mother's desire was to give me a birthday surprise that would reap lasting results, and that is God's heart as well.

SECTION *Nine*

The PRESENCE OF A MOTHER

LOOKIN' FOR JESUS IN ALL THE WRONG PLACES

WALTER WANGERIN, JR.

from *Little Lamb, Who Made Thee?*

Early in my childhood I suffered a spiritual crisis.

I can't remember now how early this was, but I was young enough to crawl beneath the church pews, small enough to be hauled back up by my mother one-handed, yet old enough to wish to see Jesus. I wanted to see Jesus with my own eyes. Ah, but I was also child enough to admit that I never truly had seen my Savior face to face. Never.

That was my crisis. Every Sunday everyone else who gathered for worship seemed so completely at ease that I was convinced they had seen God in his house. Everyone, that is, but me. They sang without distress. They prayed without regret. They nodded during sermons without a twitch of anguish, and I stared with envy into their peaceful faces. It was a party to which I alone had not been invited—in the Lord's own house, don't you see?

So who was it not inviting me?

I wanted desperately to see Christ Jesus strolling down some aisle in a robe and a rope and sandals, eating a sandwich, maybe, since I would catch him off guard, just being himself. I spent all the time between Sunday School and worship peeking into every room, the pastor's study, the roaring boiler room, seeking the signs of his presence. Nothing.

Do you think he'd hide from me? Well, I knew he knew his house better than I did. He could hide. Do you think I made him mad by some sin I couldn't even remember now? I promise, I tried with all my might to remember. But I couldn't remember one that bad. As soon as I thought of it, I was right ready to confess and be forgiven. Until then I tried to surprise the Lord in hiding.

During services I would slip down from the pew to the floor and peer among ankle-bones and pants-cuffs and shoelaces. So then, that's when my mother hauled me one-handed high onto the pew-seat again and clapped me to her side with a grip incontrovertible.

She's a very strong woman, my mother. You don't cross her. Once a forest ranger said, "If you meet a bear, you give the bear the right-of-way. Get out of there." Yeah, but my mother could silence whole congregations with a single, searing, righteous glance—so when she *did* meet that bear she beat two pans together until the bear backed down. "Woof," said the she-bear, astonished. "Not with *my* kids!" snapped my mother, uncowed. A very strong woman. Therefore I could not drop to the floor any more during worship.

But my yearning, imprisoned, increased to something like a panic.

I wanted to see Jesus!

The heart of a child is capable of great desolation and thereby of great cunning. The more I felt abandoned, the sharper became my baby wit, trying to figure where Jesus was hiding.

During one worship service, while the pastor stood facing a long wooden altar and chanting the liturgy, it dawned on me that the voice I heard was too rich to be his. This was a pale, thin preacher, but that chant charged the chancel like the King of Kings. Ha! Of course. The pastor was pretending. It was really Jesus who was chanting—Jesus, lying on his side in the altar-box, which was the size of a coffin, after all.

So, as soon as the final hymn was over and my mother's hard arm released me, I snuck forward, eyes ever on the altar to catch anyone else who might be sneaking away. Up the steps I went, right to the altar itself; and then I crept around to the side, and *YA-HA!*—I let out a loud shout to surprise the Lord in his tiny bedroom.

But nope. No Jesus. Nothing but dust and an old hymnal and a broken chair. And the angry arm of my mother, who hauled me home and caused me to sit on a bench for exactly the time of one more worship service.

The heart of a child can grow heavy with sorrow and loneliness. Why was Jesus avoiding me? Why did he take flight whenever I came near? Maybe it was my cowlick. I was not a pretty child. I knew that. Moon-faced, someone would say. Moony, generally. A daydreamer who frustrated folks who'd rather go faster. But—

But I really wanted to see Jesus. Couldn't I see Jesus too?

Which room had I never checked? Was there any such room in the church? Was there somewhere all the rest of the saints made sure I didn't see?

Yes!

Oh, my, yes! Yes! My mother didn't know how helpful had been my time on the bench. It ended in pure inspiration. There was indeed one room into which I had never gone, nor ever so much as peeped—a sanctum of terrible mystery and terrible charm. It horrified me to think of actually entering the place. It tightened my loins and made me sweat all week long, every time I contemplated venturing that door. But I would. I wanted to see Jesus, and I was convinced that this room did above all rooms qualify for a Holy of Holies. Surely he was in that place where, if a boy came in unworthily, he would die on the spot.

And so it came to pass that on the following Sunday morning I wagered my entire life on chance that I knew where the Son of God lurked. That is to say, I risked my mother's wrath. During the sermon I flat slipped from the pew, ducked her reach, skipped down the aisle and tiptoed downstairs to The Dangerous Door, The Room of Sweet Folly and Holy Violence:

Breathlessly, I approached The Women's Bathroom.

The girls' *toilet*, you understand. Boys don't ever pass it without spasms of awe.

But I was determined. And the need had made me very bold. As bold as my mother.

I knocked. I nudged the door inward.

"Jesus? Are you in there, Jesus? Jesus?"

So then my life was over.

Nothing mattered any more. I was so hopeless when I returned to my mother in her pew that I felt no fear of punishment. She could do to me as she pleased, and it would mean absolutely nothing. Jesus wasn't in there. Mirrors and wide tables and weird smells were there; but the King of Creation did not dwell in the women's bathroom. Mom could kill me for all I cared. I had looked in the last place, and the last place was empty. There was no more.

Well, no, she didn't kill me. She froze me with a glance, blue-eyed and beautiful and severe: *Just wait, young man.* So what? She pointed to the front where the pastor in black was intoning: "This cup is the New Testament in my blood. . . . ."

Blood. I guess she was indicating an ominous future for me. So what? What did I care?

"Do this in remembrance of me," said the gaunt, white, ghostly preacher, and then people began to move forward, pew by pew. They sang and they filed up the aisle.

My mother got up. She walked forward with them.

Surely I must have seen the ritual often before, but it never had had so curdling an effect on me before. I was stunned by what my mother proceeded to do.

She acted docile! In a strange humility this strong woman knelt down before the pastor. She bowed her head. And then—like a child, like a *baby*—she raised her face and let him feed her! Yo! My mother can handle me. My mother can handle the neighbors. My mother can handle black bears in the Rockies—and my mother can surely handle herself. Yet now, as meek as an infant, she accepted a cracker from the preacher's hand. Then he gave her a little drink, and she didn't even touch the cup with her hands. She sipped at his bidding. My mighty mother, brought so low! What power could have stricken her so?

Yet, when she came floating back down the aisle and into our pew, there was nothing of defeat in her face. There was a softness, rather. Pliability and private smiling. She was different.

She smelled different, too. She came in a cloud of peculiar sweetness, a rich red odor. When she sat and bowed her head to pray, I stuck my nose near her nose, whence came this scent of urgent mystery. She felt my nearness and drew back.

"Mama," I whispered, "what's that?"

"What's what?" she asked.

"That smell. What do I smell?"

"What I drank," she said.

I wanted to pull her jaw down and look into her throat. "No, but what is it?" I begged. "What's inside of you?"

"Oh, Wally," she shrugged, reaching for a hymnal, "that's Jesus. It's Jesus inside of me."

Jesus?

My mother started to sing the hymn. I stared at her. Her profile, her narrow nose, her perfectly even brow all suffused with a scent of bloody sweetness. *So that's where Jesus has been all along. In my mama!*

Who would have guessed that this was the room in the house of the Lord where the Lord most chose to dwell? In my mama. Strong woman, meek woman, a puzzle for sure. My mama.

Well, I clapped my own small self smack to her side, and I took her arm and wrapped it around me to be the closer to them I loved, and we sang, and I grinned. I beamed like sunlight.

And I know we sang a heroic *Nunc Dimittis:* "For mine eyes have seen thy salvation. . . ."

. . . in blood, in a rich red smell, in the heart of my mama.

Amen!

A DREAMER FOR THE KINGDOM

DR. ANTHONY CAMPOLO

from *What My Parents Did Right,* compiled by Gloria Gaither

She was a dreamer who never stopped dreaming. She was convinced that her life could count for Christ.

Her father died when she was just nine years old. She was the oldest of six children and, at the age of nine, went to work cleaning stores in the jewelry district of Philadelphia. Her income was the primary means of support for her impoverished immigrant family. But she had a dream. Even as a little girl, she was committed to becoming a missionary, so she went to night school. It must have been a remarkable sight in South Philadelphia, this bright-eyed, dark-skinned, Italian girl sitting in class with adult Italian immigrants as she learned to read and write.

When she was just sixteen years of age, her mother arranged a marriage for her, and all hopes of completing school ended. A girlhood friend of hers, who later went on to become a prominent American leader and a woman of letters, told me that she wept at my mother's wedding because she was convinced that this was the end of my mother's dreams. But that woman was wrong.

My mother kept on dreaming. She never got to the mission field, and she never completed her education. But she had children, and she was convinced that her dreams would be realized in her offspring. As I grew up, she told me that I was her "Samuel" and that, like that character in the Bible, I had been presented to the Lord for service. Nothing in my life motivated me to give my life to missions more than her constant reminder that she had raised me for this calling.

As I came of age, three things were prominent in her nurturing care. First, she was always there. Second, she believed in me and helped me to believe in myself. Third, she modeled for me what missionaries are supposed to be.

Living as we did in a congested and bustling city, my mother arranged with a teenage girl who lived next door to walk me home at the end of the day. For this arduous responsibility, the girl was paid five cents a day, or a grand total of a quarter a week. In second grade, I became irritated that our poor family was giving this neighbor girl so much money, and I offered a deal to my mom. "Look," I said, "I'll walk myself to school, and if you give me a nickel a week, I will be extra careful. You can keep the other twenty cents, and we'll all be better off." I pleaded and begged, and eventually my mother gave in to my proposal. For the next two years I walked to and from school all by myself. It was an eight-block walk with many streets to cross, but I crossed them all with great care. I didn't talk to any strangers. I always kept on the appointed path. I always did as I promised, and I did it alone—or at least I thought I did.

Years later when we were enjoying a family party, I bragged about my characteristic independence and, in a grandiose fashion, reminded my family of how I had been able to take care of myself even as a small boy. I recalled the arrangements for going to and from school that I had worked out with Mom. It was then that my mother laughed and told me the whole story. "Did you really think you were alone?" she asked. "Every morning when you left for school, I left with you. I walked behind you all the way. When you got out of school at 3:30 in the afternoon, I was there. I always kept myself hidden, but I was there and I followed you all the way home. I just wanted to be there for you in case you needed me."

Where can I go from your Spirit?
Where can I flee from your presence?

Psalm 139:7

THE HEMORRHAGING WOMAN

JOHN TRENT, PH.D.

from *Pictures Your Heart Remembers*

The picture is one of my favorites. You can find it framed in Luke 8. Jesus was on his way to heal a dying twelve-year-old girl, the daughter of a synagogue official named Jairus. As he was walking, the crowds were pressing against him, so the scene was fairly intense. A girl's life was at stake. An eager crowd was packed around him. And into this scene a woman with constant bleeding pushed through the crowd, thinking to herself, *If I can just get close enough to touch his garment, that will be enough.* Finally she got close enough and touched the fringe of his garment. Barely a tug. But he felt it. And he stopped. He was sensitive to the touch because it was a touch of faith. He called to her, and she came, trembling, and fell down before him. And ever so tenderly he told her, "Daughter, your faith has made you well; go in peace."

It is one of my favorite pictures because it shows me how sensitive Jesus was to the slight touch of faith we can extend to him. We don't have to have the right words. Or the right timing. Or the right anything. All we have to do is reach out to him. And he stops for us.

It's one of my favorite pictures because it reminds me of a picture of my mom—lots of pictures of my mom actually. During my senior year in high school, Jeff and I had a ritual we went through with several of our friends. After we dropped off our Saturday night dates, if we had a date, we'd meet at Jack in the Box at eleven, and together we'd wolf down an entire menu of tacos, burgers, fries, and shakes. Then about midnight, Jeff and I would head home for another ritual.

We'd walk down the hall to Mom's room, where she lay sleeping in the dark, touch her to wake her up, and then flop down on either side of her and talk about our evening—our dates, the movie we saw, the people we met. The conversation would drift to what our week had been like, what went well, what didn't. We shared our dreams, telling each other the details of our lives. Then one Saturday night, after months of this ritual, a thought struck me. "Mom?" I asked. "Does it bother you, us waking you up so late to talk?"

"Boys," she said, patting us in the dark. "I can *always* go back to sleep. But I won't always have you boys here to talk to. Wake me up anytime." And I knew she meant it. She loved us so much that she put our needs before her own. Even after midnight when she was asleep. Even when she had to get up early the next day. She was never so tired or so pressured that she couldn't talk with her boys in the dark. She always had time. *Always.*

MY FATHER'S MIRROR

CAROL WEDEVEN

For two years our daughter Rachel rode along with her younger brother, Graham, and me to bring her sister Liesl to the neighborhood nursery school. Since siblings were not allowed to stay in the car when parents brought students inside, every time we arrived, we went through the same tedious routine: unbuckle seat belts, get children out of the car, tell them to be careful—hold hands in the parking lot, avoid puddles at all costs. When we got inside, Mrs. Pope, the head teacher, greeted students, while Mrs. Zoldesy busied others with activities. We watched as Liesl hung up her coat and joined the action.

Rachel and Graham were always greeted warmly, and the teachers often encouraged Rachel to read or to play for a few minutes. Rachel usually did not want to leave, but she was too young to stay. Preschool readiness was already in full swing.

At last it was Rachel's turn to be the nursery school student. She could hardly wait. I was sure she would make a fine adjustment. She already knew the teachers, the equipment, and the routine. Only the children in her class would be new.

When we arrived on the first day, she hurried in, looked for her photo above one hook, found it, and hung up her jacket. This was her day. Thank you, God!

"Mommy," said Mrs. Pope, with Rachel near enough to hear, "remember to stay until Rachel is comfortable enough to tell you to go home."

"I will," I promised, even as I looked forward to finishing breakfast and pampering my tired feet on the couch at home (I was pregnant).

"Rachel," Mrs. Pope said, "when you're ready for Mommy to leave, you may tell her to go home."

"Okay," she said, hugging me, then running off to play.

Graham and I took a seat. It was good to take the weight off my feet for just a minute. The time could not pass quickly enough, but then I did expect to be the first mother out the door.

I chatted with other mothers, watched and waited, secretly scratching my dry, itching belly.

As Rachel piled blocks, she chatted with children and then pointed at me. *She's introducing me to the other kids,* I thought.

After twenty minutes three children told their mothers to go home. I saw Rachel peek at me from behind her tower of blocks. I'm still here, my smile said. But she did not send me home.

My back ached, and Graham was in the beginning stages of major toddler unrest. I gave him a cracker. He was quiet and happy . . . while the cracker lasted. I dreaded the end of the moment's peace. *Lord,* I prayed, *this waiting is getting to be long. Please, help me keep my promise.*

Another mother left. Another and another. Wait a minute! I thought. That's supposed to be me. What's happening?

Rachel pushed a fire truck through table legs and people legs. She waved to me as she roared past. I waved back. *Yes, honey,* my heart said, *I haven't left. I'm still here for you.* But, my body said, *I'd really like to leave now. Lord, give me patience.*

Graham wanted to join in the fun and tried to break away. I battled to keep him near me. *God, I'm uncomfortable, and slow. Help me to hold on to this quick child's hand.*

Five more children gave their mothers permission to leave. Green with envy, I watched them go. "I will never leave you nor forsake you," I heard God whisper. So I stayed put.

Rachel peered over the bookshelf. She browsed through the books, but kept one eye on me. When I waved, she pretended not to notice. Ouch! *Father, do I ignore you?*

More mothers walked out the door.

My ankles swelling by the minute, I rubbed one sore foot against the other for temporary relief. *Has she forgotten to tell me?* I thought. *I cannot believe I'm still sitting here.*

After an hour, I got Rachel's attention. She put on a fancy dress-up costume and paraded by, peeking sideways at me from the corner of her eye.

Does she need reassurance? I wondered.

"May Mommy go home now?" Mrs. Pope asked.

Rachel shook her head.

My patience was being tested . . . beyond the reasonable capacity of a very pregnant mama—in the morning. *God, I hope I don't make you wait like this. Do I test your patience?* I didn't move from my chair.

Graham ate another cracker . . . no, he ate half and dropped the other half on the floor.

I eyed the exit. So close, yet so far away. I would never have sneaked out, but, for at least two seconds, I did consider doing just that. "Keep your promise," God's Spirit whispered. "You are the Father's mirror. Rachel sees you. Your faithfulness points her to me." *Lord, help me to be faithful.*

A little later Mrs. Pope asked Rachel again, "May Mommy go home?"

Rachel shook her head again and walked away.

Graham jumped to the floor and stepped on the cracker pieces, making a mess. He objected when I tried to pick him up. I was certainly not able to bend over far enough to pick up the crumbs.

By now most mothers had been allowed to go home. I sat, one of the last bastions, on the hard wooden seat, holding a squirming boy on my lap. Lap? What lap? Christina was due to be born in a few days.

I walked Graham along the row of old chairs, or, rather, he walked me. When he discovered he could flip the seats up and down to make a loud noise, he proceeded to give each empty seat a quality check. He ran. Bang! I waddled after him. He ran farther. Bang! But before the third bang, I stopped and said in my most convincing voice, "Graham, . . ." He turned and came to be with me again. He knew my voice. *God, when I hear your voice, do I recognize it? Do I listen? turn? do your will?*

More than half the morning had passed. I knew that if I didn't get to leave soon, there would be no point in going home. I'd just have to turn around and come back for the pick-up.

My stomach growled. Even the smashed crackers on the floor started to look good. I waited, confident that keeping my promise . . . being faithful—even under uncomfortable conditions—would provide the reassurance Rachel seemed to be looking for from me.

Eventually (thankfully), Rachel did tell me to go home, or I might still be sitting there to this day. I returned to the car—Graham in tow, put him in his car seat, climbed in, clicked my seat belt, started the car, carefully exited the parking lot, and drove home to finally finish breakfast and steep a pot of tea.

As I rested my hurting back and swollen feet, with gratitude I relived my morning with God. True to his promise, he had been faithful—even before breakfast. He kept his promise to me, so that I could keep my promise to Rachel, so that she could know him better. The knowledge of God's faithfulness passed from my great-grandmother to my grandmother to my mother to me to Rachel, and today to her children, is the 24-carat gold treasure inherited by us . . . generations of God's heirs. God never leaves us, his children. He is faithful . . . 100 percent.

A HOME RUN FOR MOM

PEGGY MORRIS

Batter up!" our youth pastor yelled over the loudspeaker.

I giggled with delight as our six-foot-three-inch, sixteen-year-old son, Christopher, stepped to the plate.

This was our first church family softball tournament, and I was sitting behind home plate to encourage every batter. I had already applauded my husband and oldest son as they came through the lineup. As usual, both of them slammed the ball nearly out of the park. I screamed and yelled like a wild woman who thought their "at bats" were better than the hot dog I'd just devoured.

Now it was Chris's turn to show his stuff. The crowd cheered as he grabbed the bat with a grin on his face and positioned himself for a big hit. Chris has always been the comedian of the family. He enjoys sports, but not with the same intensity as his father and older brother. I still recall observing him during those Little League years as he stood nonchalantly in the outfield tossing his glove up in the air while the opposing team was at bat. This baseball stuff was obviously boring. We learned early on that instead of playing sports, he would much rather be acting, singing, strumming his guitar, or telling jokes.

Chris's first pitch was a swing and a miss. His second was the same. I swallowed hard as I watched the pitcher deliver the next ball.

"Strike three! You're out!" announced our youth pastor.

Did he have to broadcast it in to the microphone? I wondered, as Chris walked toward the dugout seemingly taking his strikeout in stride.

Before long Chris was up to bat for the second time. Once again he struck out. He tried to smile, but I could sense he was upset as he listlessly walked away from home plate. I felt like I needed to run out there, hug him, and soothe the hurt like I did when he was a little boy. I wanted to reassure him that strikeouts have nothing to do with his value as a person.

191

As I sat there in my chair, I could feel my heart beating in my throat. While the game continued, all I could think was, *Is Chris all right?*

I wrestled with the idea of sneaking behind the dugout to talk to him, but instead I plastered on a smile and decided to suppress my emotions, especially since I was surrounded on all sides.

Later that evening, when all the fun and frivolity had ended, Chris drove his Dad and me home. I noticed that he wasn't his usual jovial self. I wanted so badly to do something, to say something, anything to cheer him up, but I knew the timing wasn't right. It's not always easy to know exactly what to say as the parent of a teenager. I had messed up plenty of times before, and I was determined not to blow this one.

When we arrived home, Chris went to his room. I knew he wanted to be left alone for a while. I understood, because when I feel sad, it's good for me to take a few minutes by myself to process through my emotions. I prayed that God would speak to Chris's heart and reassure him how special he is. So often God comforts me like that when I feel misunderstood or useless.

Later that night as I prepared Chris's lunch for the next school day, the thought came to me to write him a note of encouragement and tape it to his sandwich bag. I often do this for my family to reassure them of my love and to remind them that they're in my prayers. So I wrote a little note, which simply read:

You're a great son. I love you. And I'm proud of you. —Mom

The next day as I arrived to pick Chris up after school, I couldn't believe it when I spotted him standing head and shoulders above the crowd with my note taped to the front of his shirt. I laughed and felt like crying at the same time as Chris approached the car with the biggest grin on his face I've ever seen. I wanted to take my hands off the wheel and squeeze him when he said, "I found the note in my lunch, and I loved it so much I decided to wear it all day."

As he plopped his backpack onto the seat, he exclaimed, "Everyone thought my note was great, Mom! Even this rough, tough guy in my math class said he liked it and wished his Mom would write him one like that!"

As I reflect on that incident, I can clearly see how valuable Chris is to me whether he becomes a big slugger or not. He's my son, and he's God's child. And on that particular day he hit a home run that will live forever in my heart.

A NIGHT FOR REMEMBERING

JAN POTTER

I'm coming, I'm coming!" I groaned, sitting up in bed. I finally realized the high-pitched howling that invaded my dream was not a fire engine, but my five-year-old daughter.

I dreaded the icy chill that awaited me when the covers were off and my feet hit the floor, but better to brave the cold than risk waking everyone in the house. Yawning and fumbling with my robe, I shuffled into Kristi's room and plopped down on her bed.

"Honey, what's wrong?" I whispered.

"Tummy hurts . . . tummy hurts," she whined.

I sat for a moment debating my plan of action. Should I give her baby aspirin and tell her to go back to sleep or rock her? I decided on the latter, hoping to catch a wink or two myself. Gathering up my distressed child, her blanket, and teddy, I carried her into the living room.

"This vinyl rocker is cold at 1:30 in the morning!" I shivered. Kristi stopped crying as she snuggled on my lap, and I rested my cheek on top of her head, gently rocking back and forth.

Mesmerized by the steady creaking of the platform rocker, I began to drift into another dream world. I envisioned a little girl in her mother's lap, rocking and listening to soothing lullabies. I began humming "Rock-a-bye-baby" as I remembered being that little girl twenty-plus years before.

I had felt warm and protected there on Mother's lap. As memories flooded my mind, my senses even picked up that certain fragrance Mom always had about her. It was a good mother-scent—sometimes her Tussy cream deodorant, sometimes bath powder that she generously doused on daily, and sometimes the aroma of freshly baked cookies or chocolate cake lingered after her.

Mom always rushed around adding another load to the washer, boiling handkerchiefs, making beds, meals, and music. With a husband and four children, her work never seemed to end. She usually went to bed last and got up before anyone else. We didn't need alarm clocks. The aroma of bacon, eggs, and pancakes, and Mom calling out "Breakfast!" woke us up in the morning. I thought about those special Saturday nights, year after year, when Mom stayed up past midnight sewing new Easter dresses for my sister and me.

When sickness struck, Mom sprang into action with her home remedies. Whenever we started to sniffle or get a sore throat, she "greased" our noses good! I remember waking up many nights to the smell of Mentholatum and the feel of a rough, dishpan forefinger rubbing it on my nose and around my neck. I chuckled, thinking back to the night, as Mom so often told the story, when she heard one of us sneeze. She bounded out of bed and pulled the good old cure-all Mentholatum out of her dresser drawer. Not knowing who sneezed, she efficiently gave us all the treatment and returned to bed. The next morning we wandered in to her, asking, "Mom, what's this white stuff all over our noses?" Mom laughed, realizing that in the dark she had accidentally grabbed her jar of deodorant!

Yes, I thought, Mother sacrificed her right to stay in a warm, comfortable bed many times. She served unselfishly, uncomplaining.

"I feel better, Mommy," Kristi's voice jarred me back to the present.

"Do you want to go back to bed now?" I asked.

She yawned and nodded.

Her response actually disappointed me. I was having such a good time reminiscing. I wondered if Kristi will remember me this way in years to come as she rocks her child's hurts away. My mother taught me something that night, even though she lived seven hundred miles away.

Kristi sauntered away, dragging her blanket, then suddenly stopped, turned around, and said, "Thank you, Mommy."

"You're sure welcome, honey," I said with surprise. "I love you."

"I love you, Mommy."

I read on a plaque that "God couldn't be everywhere, so He made mothers." Of course that isn't true. God IS everywhere. But maybe he did make mothers to help carry out his plans for us to be loved and comforted; to be the physical, human hands and voices that tell us he cares deeply for us and will always meet our needs. I know I can call on the Lord anytime day or night because he is always available, just as my mother was there for me so many years ago.

SECTION *Ten*

The UNCONDITIONAL
LOVE OF A MOTHER

ON LOVE

MOTHER TERESA

from *No Greater Love*

L et us understand the tenderness of God's love. For He speaks in the Scripture, "Even if a mother could forget her child, I will not forget you. I have carved you on the palm of my hand" (see Isaiah 49:15-16). When you feel lonely, when you feel unwanted, when you feel sick and forgotten, remember you are precious to Him. He loves you. Show that love for one another, for this is all that Jesus came to teach us.

I remember a mother of twelve children, the last of them terribly mutilated. It is impossible for me to describe that creature. I volunteered to welcome the child into our house, where there are many others in similar conditions. The woman began to cry. "For God's sake, Mother," she said, "don't tell me that. This creature is the greatest gift of God to me and my family. All our love is focused on her. Our lives would be empty if you took her from us." Hers was a love full of understanding and tenderness. Do we have a love like that today? Do we realize that our child, our husband, our wife, our father, our mother, our sister or brother, has a need for that understanding, for the warmth of our hand?

I will never forget one day in Venezuela when I went to visit a family who had given us a lamb. I went to thank them and there I found out that they had a badly crippled child. I asked the mother, "What is the child's name?" The mother gave me a most beautiful answer. "We call him 'Teacher of Love,' because he keeps on teaching us how to love. Everything we do for him is our love for God in action."

We have a great deal of worth in the eyes of God. I never tire of saying over and over again that God loves us. It is a wonderful thing that God Himself loves me tenderly. That is why we should have courage, joy, and the conviction that nothing can separate us from the love of Christ.

THE FEAR OF LOSS

SHEILA WALSH

from *Living Fearlessly*

n *Mere Christianity*, C. S. Lewis quotes a schoolboy who was asked what God is like. The boy replied, "The sort of person who is always snooping around to see if anyone is enjoying himself, and then trying to stop it." A funny answer, perhaps, but at some core level many of us share this fear. We think, *This is too good. Life is too smooth. God is going to throw a wrench in the works at any moment.* Perhaps this is why Paul urged the members of the church in Philippi to "continue to work out [their] salvation with fear and trembling" (Philippians 2:12). It's a scary business to trust God with total abandon. "Fear and trembling" are not popular words. I'd much rather have joy and hope. Or laughter and mercy. But fear and trembling? Not good PR words.

I joined the Women of Faith team in February of 1997, when Christian was just six weeks old. I knew Barbara Johnson's story because I'd interviewed her on *The 700 Club*. But I had become a mommy since then. As I sat onstage for the first time and heard her enumerate the tragedies that had decimated her life, I was horrified. I was the new kid on the block, so I had to behave and look borderline sane, but I could have laid on the floor of the arena and sobbed.

Barbara talked about her husband, Bill, and his car accident. He wasn't expected to live. He'd sustained a severe brain injury, which had left him blind. But God has healed him. As Bill walked onstage to say hello, we all cheered and whistled. Then Barb moved on to the death of her son Steven. He had been killed in Vietnam, and because of Bill's condition at the time, she had to go identify the body by herself. I tried to control myself, but I felt as if someone had grabbed hold of my heart with an iron fist and was squeezing the life out of it. I felt sick.

Then she told us about the car wreck that took the life of her son Tim. It was five years to the day when she went once again to identify the body of one of her boys in a funeral home. Bill could have gone this time, but she wanted to spare him the nightmare picture that was etched into her mind and heart from identifying Steven the first time around. It was unspeakable.

"You really need the grace of God when you stand and look at what's left of your firstborn son, delivered from Canada in pieces in an orange crate," she said.

I sat with my head in my hands and sobbed. The thought of this ever happening to my little boy was more than I could bear.

Barbara kept on going. When her third son became estranged from the family, disappearing into the homosexual subculture for eleven years, Barb contemplated taking her life. But then she said something that surprised me. Finally, she said, after a year of grief so intense she could barely function, she prayed what she calls the prayer of relinquishment: "Whatever, Lord! Whatever you bring into my life, it's all right. Like Job said, 'Though he slay me, yet will I hope in him' " (Job 13:15).

Everyone applauded this great statement of surrender from this remarkable woman whom I have come to love like I love my own mother. But I wanted to run off the stage, out of the building, and off the team. It was too much for me. All my worst fears came rushing to the surface.

Is God going to do that to me so that I can have a great, victorious story to tell from the stage? I wondered in horror. *If so, I'm going to get a job at Wal-Mart.* And I really meant it. All right, perhaps Nordstrom.

I talked to Barbara later that day at the hotel and told her how I felt. She said to me, "Sheila, you're trying to put yourself in my shoes but without the grace God gave me, without the huge 'comfort blanket' of love he wrapped me in. When I left the funeral home after identifying Tim's remains, God gave me an incredible gift. I looked up into the sky, and I saw Tim's face smiling down at me. That kind of thing is not in my Baptist background, but I sure needed it. He said, 'Don't cry, Mom, I'm not there. I'm worshiping Jesus around the throne of grace.' "

"I think that's awesome, Barb," I said. "But I want Christian here with me."

"I know," she said, as she gave me a hug. "I wanted Tim too."

As I put Christian to bed that night in our hotel room, I sat beside his crib for a while, watching him as he slept. I wanted to imprint every image of him into my soul. I listened to the little noises he makes with his mouth when he's sleeping. His lips move as if he is planting little kisses on God's cheek. He had a lot of hair for a six-week-old baby, and it curled round his ears. I leaned over and smelled his neck. He smelled like summer.

When Barry fell asleep, I took a bath. As I lay in the tub I poured my heart out to God: *I feel like I'm in a wrestling match here, Lord, and you're bigger. You're going to win. I know you've given everything to me. I know you gave me your own Son, so surely you understand how hard this is. I want to trust you more. I want to. You'll need to teach me how, though, for I don't have a clue.*

I picked up my Bible, which I now keep in the bathroom so I can take advantage of a few quiet moments alone with the Lord, and I read these words: "Are you tired? Worn out? Burned out on religion? Come to me. On vacation with me, you'll recover your life. I'll show you how to take a real rest. Walk with me and work with me—watch how I do it. Learn the unforced rhythms of grace. I won't lay anything heavy or ill-fitting on you. Keep company with me and you'll learn to live freely and lightly" Matthew 11:28–29, (THE MESSAGE).

"Thank you, Lord," I whispered, tears streaming down my face. I climbed out of the tub and went to sleep.

GOING HOME

BARBARA JOHNSON

from Where Does a Mother Go to Resign?

Background: On a hot Saturday in June, 1975, Barbara Johnson had planned a family outing at Disneyland. As she was leaving for the park, the phone rang. One of her son's friends was calling, asking to borrow a book. While searching through her son's bookcase, she happened upon some homosexual material. Later that day, at Disneyland, she confronted her son, Larry, with her discovery. He confirmed her fears. Larry moved out of the house and Barbara didn't hear from him for eleven months. Barbara spent those months in learning how to love her son unconditionally—a word that took on a whole new realm of meaning for her. The story you are about to read is part of her journal—"progress notes," as she calls them.

Today started out like any typical busy Saturday. The gardener was pruning the camelias, the pool man was there cleaning the pool, and my heart was still really singing from the lifting of the burden two days ago at Melodyland.

When the phone rang, I expected it to be my friend who was going with me to visit a new mall which is just opening this week. Instead, I heard a familiar voice, one which I had missed for eleven months, saying, "I'm at In-n-Out Hamburgs, and I'd like to bring you a hamburg. What would you like on it?" This voice from the past had its usual cheeriness, the usual boyish sound—and yet sort of hesitant.

For a fraction of a second, I thought of all the things I wanted to do which would be the right things! I didn't want to cry or sound too emotional. I wanted to let Larry know that I was glad to hear from him, and yet not sound too glad so that he would be afraid of an emotional scene if he came home. But of course there was so much excitement and emotion welling up within me that I found it hard to muster a normal-sounding voice to just say, "Oh, anything you get is fine." Larry used to work at that particular hamburger place and knew from experience what I wanted on my hamburgers; but calling was, I think, his way of determining my attitude toward him after so many months of silence.

Hanging up the phone, I sat as though paralyzed for a minute. It would take him about twenty minutes to get home, and in that time I had to run through the house and get all the gay literature and books I had been studying and collecting out of sight. I didn't want him to be turned off by the fact that I was so obviously making a real study of this subject. I dashed through each room and threw everything that even looked like it hinted of homosexuality under the bed! (*I was hiding gay literature from* him?)

Then I called Frank with the desperate question: "What shall I do? *Larry is coming to see me!*" How can I act sort of aloof when inside I want to hold him like I'll never let go? How can I treat him as an adult and not show any motherly concern? Is there a special button you push that suddenly changes a longtime mother into just a friend to her child? Frank's calm advice helped me to gather my wits together.

Larry's picture was still up on the piano where it had been since he left. I had turned it around for several months because I couldn't bear to look at it and wonder where he was. But it was dusted off, and I knew that when he came in the door and saw his picture in its usual place on the piano, it would signal to him that he was still our son—still loved, still accepted, still part of the family.

After surveying the house and seeing that all was in order for his arrival, I had this sudden, wild impulse to find a baby doll, wrap it all up in a blanket, and then when he came in and asked what's new, I could say, "Well, you have a two-month-old baby sister." After all, he had been gone almost a year and anything could have happened! (It was a far-out idea—but then for him to be coming home was pretty far out too!)

Just then the moment came. I heard Larry struggling with the front door; then he walked in, spilling fries all over the entryway in his efforts to balance the hamburgers, fries and Cokes. I merely said lighthearted things like, "What do you do for an encore, Larry?" (after he had succeeded in spilling the remainder of the fries on the carpet). I was praying desperately that I would not appear too emotional or cry. I was actually thankful for this little *faux pas* of his, so we could concentrate on talking about wet, soggy hamburgers and picking up french fries from the white brick entryway. Small talk can be such a blessing when you are exploding inside.

We collected what was left of the "lunch" and spread it out on the kitchen table. Just Larry and me for the first time in eleven months. I hugged him and told him how good he looked and how glad I was to see him. The dog sniffed him and wagged his tail but wasn't sure who he was, either, at this point. Sitting there, talking of mundane things such as how much the flowers had grown, and how the dog was doing, and how much easier it was to care for the new tile on the kitchen floor was somewhat difficult for me. I had so many questions, but I let him carry the ball in the conversation. He seemed eager to talk—not about anything special, just sort of catching up on what we had been doing. I followed Frank's advice and didn't pump him for any information, and the atmosphere was not as tense as I had been prepared for. Actually, it was as if Larry had been on a long, long trip (to the moon, maybe) and had come home, showing a great interest in what had happened at the house while he was gone. He stayed about an hour and played the piano a bit. It was so good to hear him play some old favorites of his. He loves Bach and the classics, and is exceptionally good at the piano. The pins and needles I had experienced before he came sort of disappeared. It was as if all the separation and pain was like the anguish of child-birth—forgotten when it is behind you.

Perhaps the lifting of my spirit two days ago had been God's special way of wrapping me in His love so that I could show that love to Larry without any traces of resentment or the questions which normally would have spilled out.

I hugged Larry and told him how much we loved him. There was no mention of homosexuality or his lifestyle or where he was living or what he was doing. I knew that any probing would have to be gentle, and it would be difficult to come across with a gentle probe when I wanted so much more information. So I just asked the Lord for an opportunity to use the patience I had learned in the past year. (Patience is the ability to idle your motor when you feel like stripping your gears. And, believe me, I had learned to idle the motor by this time!) Larry didn't seem in a hurry to leave; he took a run through the rest of the house and checked over his room. You would have thought he was from the building and code department by the way he so carefully inspected everything.

Then, being as light as possible, we had some cola and sat in the living room and talked about some neighborhood changes, about the fact that my car had been painted, about the tree in front having been removed because the roots were entwined in the water lines—at least we were *talking*! We were communicating not on the subject I wanted to talk about—but this was his day. Since I knew my probes would be too deep and the surgery or wounds were still visible, I would just let him overflow with his thoughts and keep mine tightly zipped up until I had sorted out my feelings myself.

When Larry left, we hugged each other and I said I loved him. His face showed some real expression of appreciation that he had made this initial contact with me. He said he'd come back and see his dad and brother soon. He had borrowed a car to come over, and when he left I stood on the porch and waved him off (which is our usual custom). I waited a minute, as the little car headed down the street, and then I was thrilled to hear the familiar three short blasts from the horn—a special little family signal meaning "I love you."

So funny, that three short honks would send me into such ecstasy! The relief of seeing him, knowing he was okay, and knowing that he honked that horn three times meant to me that he had made a big step in the healing for which our family had been praying for almost a year.

I sat alone and cried for a while; but they were tears of relief and of joy. When words fail, tears flow. And words surely failed me in those moments. Nothing I did to restrain the flow helped. It was as if all the bound-up feelings and buried restraints were being released at the same time. My emotional "hose" was getting flushed out and a real catharsis was taking place.

According to Psalm 56:8, God puts our tears in His bottle and enters them into the record He keeps of our lives. I had read that verse in the past and now I am reflecting on how many buckets of tears I must have cried since our devastating night at Disneyland.

Barbara Johnson founded Spatula Ministries, a non-profit organization designed to "peel parents off the ceiling with a spatula of love and begin them on the road to recovery."

COLOR ME MAD!

MARLENE BAGNULL

O h, Mommy," my little girl exclaimed as she threw her arms around me, "I love my room."

I hugged her, feeling a warm glow inside. It had cost more than we could afford to surprise her with a new bedspread and curtains for her ninth birthday; but seeing the look in her eyes, I knew it was worth every cent. The powder-blue gingham spread with its delicate flowers looked beautiful with the contrasting ruffled sheers on her windows. Her plain bedroom had been transformed into the kind of room I had always longed for when I was a young girl.

"You'll have to take good care of the bedspread," I said.

She solemnly nodded and promised she would.

Several weeks later I almost fell over when I opened her bedroom door. Her pretty new spread was covered with vibrant shades of yellow, blue, green, and red. I dropped the laundry basket. "Kathie, come here!" I screamed.

"What do you want?" she asked in a timid voice.

"What do I want? What happened to your bedspread?"

Kathie looked down at the floor and nervously shifted her weight from one foot to the other.

"I don't know," she mumbled.

"What do you mean, 'I don't know'? Did you or did you not do this?"

Kathie didn't need to reply. Her face revealed her guilt.

"Why? Whatever possessed you to do such a thing?"

"I was coloring with my new markers and—"

"And?"

"And I guess some got on the bedspread."

"Some! It's covered with lines and doodles." I took a deep breath and closed my eyes, praying for self-control. "This was no accident. You did it deliberately. But why? I thought you loved your new bedspread."

She began to sob. "I do. I—I don't know why I did it. I'm sorry."

Angrily I pulled the bedspread off the bed, hoping I could get out the stains. I slammed the door behind me. I would talk to her later when I had figured out an appropriate punishment.

Neither the first nor second washing made any difference in the intensity of the colors. A friend brought over the cleaning fluid she uses to get printer's ink out of her husband's work clothes. It made the marks and the entire bedspread a shade lighter.

Dinnertime felt more like ulcer-time as I told my husband what his daughter had done. He shook his head in exasperation.

Kathie's chin trembled. "How are you going to punish me?"

"I don't know," her dad said. "Maybe the fact that your bedspread is ruined is punishment enough."

A large tear rolled down her face. I wanted to kiss it away, but I was still too angry and upset. Besides, I told myself, Kathie needed "tough love" more than my sympathy.

I half-listened to the television that evening. I couldn't get my mind off what had happened. Why would my youngster do such a dumb thing? I had thought Kathie was a mature child. Certainly a nine-year-old should have been beyond such destructiveness.

"I really don't know why I did it," Kathie said as I tucked her into bed. "I'm sorry."

I didn't know what to say, so I didn't say anything as I walked out of her bedroom and closed the door.

"God give me wisdom," I prayed as I crawled into bed several hours later, but sleep wouldn't come.

Suddenly I remembered instances when I had said words similar to my daughter's.

"God, I don't know why I was so irritable with the children." . . . "I don't know why I listened to that gossip, even joined in." . . . "I don't know why I let my temper get the best of me."

All at once I had a glimpse into the heart of God. I saw the way I often grieved him more than this episode with my little girl had grieved me. After all,

I'm an adult. I know God's Word. I know right from wrong. I have the power of his Spirit to help me choose what is right. Yet still, not meaning or wanting to, I disappoint him so often.

Tears flowed down my cheeks as I thought of the countless times God had forgiven me and how I had failed to forgive my daughter.

"God, I'm sorry," I said as I climbed out of bed and went into Kathie's room. She stirred as I bent down to kiss her.

"I love you," I whispered.

"I love you, too," she said as she wrapped her arms around my neck. "Are you still angry with me for ruining my bedspread?"

"No, Kathie," I replied. "Sometimes I also do things I regret and don't even understand. I do the opposite of what I really want to do. But do you know what?"

"What?" she sniffled.

"God always forgives me when I'm sorry. He never stops loving me, and he will never stop loving you no matter what you do. And I'll never stop loving you either."

SOMEONE ELSE'S CHILD

JANICE THOMPSON

She wasn't our daughter, though it might have taken more than a glance to establish the fact. She bore the same shiny chestnut hair, the same rosy complexion, and a sense of humor that rivaled that of each of our own three daughters. But she wasn't our daughter. She was someone else's child.

We first met Courtney when she was thirteen. She was a neighborhood kid. She was new to the youth group at church, and my kids had taken a liking to her. Courtney wasn't exactly the kind of teen that a parent would be drawn to immediately. In fact, she was plenty rough around the edges. She was streetwise, having already experienced more of life than our three daughters put together. Our own girls, fifteen, seventeen, and eighteen at the time, had lived fairly sheltered lives.

I often asked my daughters about Courtney: "Who is she? What are her parents like? Where, exactly, does she live?" The fact that she kept showing up at our door, day after day, was a clear indication that all was not well at home. But I hadn't met her parents, and I really knew very little about this child who was rapidly becoming "one of mine." Who was this little waif, and why did she have such a desire to be with us? Why had she taken to calling me "Mom" and treating my own girls more like sisters than friends?

Courtney's story unraveled, not slowly, as some threads seem to do—but rather abruptly one night. She had just returned home after spending a full day with us when the telephone rang. I answered to a tearful Courtney, more frightened little girl than brave young woman. Her voice was laced with panic.

"Mom, my dad is . . . sick. Can you come and drive him to the hospital?"

I quickly found my way to their house and watched as her dad, frail and thin, got into my car. He looked gravely ill. A very shaken Courtney climbed into the backseat. As we made our way to the hospital, he began to pour out his heart. I learned, much to my shock, that he was not suffering from the stomach flu, as Courtney had suggested, but from alcohol poisoning. He had apparently struggled with alcoholism for years.

I don't know if it was the alcohol or the fear of impending death, but this man, a complete stranger, spoke to me as though I were a friend. He told me of Courtney's mother, who had left him when Courtney was five years old, never to be seen or heard from again. He spoke of a faith in God that he clutched to despite his situation. He bragged about Courtney, his precious little girl who had walked hand in hand with him down this rocky road.

I peered into the rearview mirror at Courtney's tearstained face and suddenly understood everything. She wasn't a child. She only bore the body of one. Her heart and soul were tainted with the realities of a grown-up world. Her eyes sought mine in the mirror. They met with silent understanding. She needed me. She needed *us*.

Courtney's father was rushed to the hospital in critical condition several times that summer. In fact, his battle continued longer than anticipated. Days turned into weeks, and then months. Courtney's dad waffled from one extreme to the other—frequenting every Intensive Care Unit in town and finally ending up in jail for driving while intoxicated. All the while, Courtney remained with us. As a family, we prayed that God would heal her father—but we also recognized that the decision to quit drinking had to be his.

It was a cool October evening when Courtney's father came to us, asking the inevitable question: "Would you keep Courtney for a year so that I can enter a treatment facility?"

We happily agreed. He signed a Power of Attorney that night, and Courtney came to live with us. Legally.

Sadly, her father checked himself out of the facility after only four months. He wandered from state to state, looking for work, looking for peace. In a moment of desperation, he arrived at a Christian facility accustomed to dealing with men in his condition. He checked himself in, but stayed only a few weeks before moving on.

Courtney has become a happy, well-adjusted seventeen-year-old, whose most current concern is whether or not she will get to drive soon. She has had to struggle through the battles that a child of an alcoholic faces, but is conquering them all with God's help. She has recommitted her life to Christ. Courtney is part of the worship team in her youth group, attends a Christian school, and played a starring role in a school drama production. She is completely "family" now—arguing and bickering on occasion, just like our other girls. She has a laugh that could turn any frown upside down. All in all, she is pure delight.

Courtney writes her dad often, and he sends childhood photos, a signal that he is thinking of her, loving her.

When I overhear people talking about Courtney, I am reminded of how far we've all come together.

"She's someone else's child," I hear them whisper.

I correct them quickly.

"No," I respond, looking them squarely in the eye. "She is our daughter."

COME HOME

MAX LUCADO

from *No Wonder They Call Him the Savior*

The practice of using earthly happenings to clarify heavenly truths is no easy task. Yet, occasionally, one comes across a story, legend, or fable that conveys a message as accurately as a hundred sermons and with ten times the creativity. Such is the case with the reading below. I heard it first told by a Brazilian preacher in Sao Paulo. And though I've shared it countless times, with each telling I am newly warmed and reassured by its message.

The small house was simple but adequate. It consisted of one large room on a dusty street. Its red-tiled roof was one of many in this poor neighborhood on the outskirts of the Brazilian village. It was a comfortable home. Maria and her daughter, Christina, had done what they could to add color to the gray walls and warmth to the hard dirt floor: an old calendar, a faded photograph of a relative, a wooden crucifix. The furnishings were modest: a pallet on either side of the room, a washbasin, and a wood-burning stove.

Maria's husband had died when Christina was an infant. The young mother, stubbornly refusing opportunities to remarry, got a job and set out to raise her young daughter. And now, fifteen years later, the worst years were over. Though Maria's salary as a maid afforded few luxuries, it was reliable and it did provide food and clothes. And now Christina was old enough to get a job to help out.

Some said Christina got her independence from her mother. She recoiled at the traditional idea of marrying young and raising a family. Not that she couldn't have had her pick of husbands. Her olive skin and brown eyes kept a steady stream of prospects at her door. She had an infectious way of throwing her head back and filling the room with laughter. She also had that rare magic some women have that makes every man feel like a king just by being near them. But it was her spirited curiosity that made her keep all the men at arm's length.

212

She spoke often of going to the city. She dreamed of trading her dusty neighborhood for exciting avenues and city life. Just the thought of this horrified her mother. Maria was always quick to remind Christina of the harshness of the streets. "People don't know you there. Jobs are scarce and the life is cruel. And besides, if you went there, what would you do for a living?"

Maria knew exactly what Christina would do, or would *have* to do for a living. That's why her heart broke when she awoke one morning to find her daughter's bed empty. Maria knew immediately where her daughter had gone. She also knew immediately what she must do to find her. She quickly threw some clothes in a bag, gathered up all her money, and ran out of the house.

On her way to the bus stop she entered a drugstore to get one last thing. Pictures. She sat in the photograph booth, closed the curtain, and spent all she could on pictures of herself. With her purse full of small black-and-white photos, she boarded the next bus to Rio de Janeiro.

Maria knew Christina had no way of earning money. She also knew that her daughter was too stubborn to give up. When pride meets hunger, a human will do things that were before unthinkable. Knowing this, Maria began her search. Bars, hotels, nightclubs, any place with the reputation for street walkers or prostitutes. She went to them all. And at each place she left her picture—taped on a bathroom mirror, tacked to a hotel bulletin board, fastened to a corner phone booth. And on the back of each photo she wrote a note.

It wasn't too long before both the money and the pictures ran out, and Maria had to go home. The weary mother wept as the bus began its long journey back to her small village.

It was a few weeks later that young Christina descended the hotel stairs. Her young face was tired. Her brown eyes no longer danced with youth but spoke of pain and fear. Her laughter was broken. Her dream had become a nightmare. A thousand times over she had longed to trade these countless beds for her secure pallet. Yet the little village was, in too many ways, too far away.

As she reached the bottom of the stairs, her eyes noticed a familiar face. She looked again, and there on the lobby mirror was a small picture of her mother. Christina's eyes burned and her throat tightened as she walked across the room and removed the small photo. Written on the back was this compelling invitation. "Whatever you have done, whatever you have become, it doesn't matter. Please come home."

She did.

PERMISSIONS AND ACKNOWLEDGMENTS

Every effort was made to secure proper permission and acknowledgment for each story in this work. If an error has been made, please accept my apologies and contact Bethany House Publishers at 11400 Hampshire Ave. S., Minneapolis, MN 55438 so that corrections can be made in future editions.

Permission to reprint any of the stories from this work must be obtained from the original source. Acknowledgments are listed by story title in the order they appear in the book. Heartfelt thanks to all the authors and publishers who allowed their work to be included in this collection.

The Wisdom of a Mother
"I Would Give My Child the Gift of Friendship," excerpted from *Friends Through Thick and Thin,* by Sue Buchanan; Joy MacKenzie; Gloria L. Gaither; Peggy Benson. Copyright © 1998 by Gloria Gaither; Sue Buchanan; Peggy Benson; Joy MacKenzie. Used by permission of Zondervan. All rights reserved.
"The Cassette Tape," by Beth Moore, excerpted from *Feathers From My Nest* (Broadman and Holman Publishers, 2001), 169–174. All rights reserved. Used by permission.
"The Day Mama Baked the Bird," by Clint Kelly. Copyright © 2002. Used by permission. All rights reserved. Clint Kelly is a novelist, magazine freelancer, and a communications specialist for Seattle Pacific University. He and his wife, Cheryll, have four children and make their home in Everett, Washington. Clint is a card-carrying member of the Fellowship of Merry Christians, a group of comedians his mom would have loved.
"The Candy Bar Wars," by Douglas Knox. Copyright © 2002. Used by permission. All rights reserved. Doug Knox is a freelance writer from Ashland, Ohio. He edits the Christian Web site www.ChristianRoadsMinistries.usclargo.com and is working on his first novel. In his spare time he conducts fieldwork for a creation-science foundation. He and his wife, Marie, are members of Faith Christian Fellowship, a new church outreach.
"I've Discovered the Benefits of Biting My Tongue," taken from *Confessions of Four Friends Through Thick and Thin,* by Sue Buchanan; Joy MacKenzie; Gloria L. Gaither; Peggy Benson. Copyright © 2001 by Gloria Gaither;

Peggy Benson; Sue Buchanan; Joy MacKenzie. Used by permission of Zondervan. All rights reserved.

"Teaching Grandma," by Jean Davis. Copyright © 2002. Used by permission. All rights reserved. Jean Davis has published poetry and devotionals and is currently working on her second novel. She is a member of Delmarva Christian Writers' Fellowship and also Story Writers.

The Prayers of a Mother

"Fervent Love," by Patrick Borders. Copyright © 2002. Used by permission. All rights reserved. Patrick Borders lives outside Atlanta, Georgia, with his wife, Tonya, and two children, Lauren and Jared. In addition to being a stay-at-home dad, he is a freelance writer, whose work has appeared in *Guideposts.*

"Losing Jeff," excerpted from *Psalms for the Single Mom.* Copyright © 1999 by Lisa Hussey. Copied with permission from Cook Communications Ministries. May not be further reproduced. All rights reserved.

"The Faith of a Mother's Prayer," excerpted from *The Eyes of the Heart,* by Tracie Peterson. Copyright © 2002 by Tracie Peterson. Used by permission of Bethany House Publishers. All rights reserved.

"A Mother's Prayer," by Rachel Wallace-Oberle. Copyright © 2002. Used by permission. All rights reserved. Rachel Wallace-Oberle has an education in Radio/Television Broadcasting as well as Journalism/Print. She is a freelance writer and has written for numerous publications. One of her favorite topics to write about is her family. She also co-hosts a weekly Christian radio program. In her spare time, Rachel loves walking, classical music, and canaries.

"I Realize I've Been Praying Wrong My Whole Life," taken from *Confessions of Four Friends Through Thick And Thin,* by Sue Buchanan; Joy MacKenzie; Gloria L. Gaither; Peggy Benson. Copyright © 2001 by Gloria Gaither; Peggy Benson; Sue Buchanan; Joy MacKenzie. Used by permission of Zondervan. All rights reserved.

"Growing Pains," by Suzy Ryan. Copyright © 2002. Used by permission. All rights reserved. Suzy Ryan's writing has been published in numerous magazine and newspaper articles. She lives with her family in Southern California.

The Example of a Mother

"To Soar Again," by Linda Knight. Copyright © 2002. Used by permission. All rights reserved. Linda Knight is the author of more than two thousand greeting card verses. Her poetry can be found in card shops around the world. She resides with her husband in Woodslee, Ontario, Canada.

"Mom, Mers, and Mrs. Grubb," by Bob Hostetler. Copyright © 2002. Used by permission. All rights reserved. Bob Hostetler is an award-winning writer whose books include *Don't Check Your Brains at the Door* (co-authored with Josh McDowell) and *They Call Me A.W.O.L.* He lives in Hamilton, Ohio, with his wife, Robin, and two children.

"Time for One More Hand?" by Kay Shostak. Copyright © 2002. Used by permission. All rights reserved. Kay Dew Shostak, like her mother before her, has three children. She and her husband, Mike, are raising them in Marietta, Georgia, where Kay spends her mornings writing. She is currently seeking publication of her first fiction book, a contemporary story set in a farming community outside Chicago.

"Waving at Miss Velma," by Lanita Bradley Boyd. Copyright © 2002. Used by permission. All rights reserved. Lanita Bradley Boyd, a freelance writer in Fort Thomas, Kentucky, draws from years of teaching, church ministry, and family experiences. She has three stories in the *God Allows U-Turns* series and articles in a variety of publications, including *Teaching K–8, Christian Woman*, and *Parent Life.*

"A Purse Full of Love and Wonder," by Anita Higman. Copyright © 2002. Used by permission. All rights reserved. Anita Higman has been honored as a Barnes & Noble "Author of the Month" for Houston. She writes both fiction and nonfiction, and her fifteenth book will be released in 2003. Ms. Higman has won two awards for her contribution to literacy, as well as winning a Westerners International "Best Book" award for one of her coauthored books.

"Christmas," excerpted from *The Proverbs 31 Lady and Other Impossible Dreams* by Marsha Drake. Copyright © 1984 by Marsha Drake. Used by permission of Bethany House Publishers. All rights reserved.

The Grace of a Mother

"The Lemonade Stand," excerpted from *Second Row, Piano Side,* by Chonda Pierce. Copyright © 1996 by Beacon Hill Press of Kansas City. Used by permission. All rights reserved.

"Perfectly Adapted," from *A Path Through Suffering,* by Elisabeth Elliot © 1990 by Elisabeth Elliot Gren. Published by Servant Publications, P.O. Box 8617, Ann Arbor, Michigan, 48107. Used by permission. All rights reserved. Permission also granted for non-exclusive English Language rights to countries not covered by Servant's grant of permission by Lars Gren.

"A Priceless Gift," by Meghan J. Rossi. Copyright © 2002. Used by permission. All rights reserved. Meghan Johanna Rossi will be forever grateful for her mom's living example of grace during times of crisis and to her heavenly Father for providing such an example when she needed it the most. Meghan lives in the Midwest with her husband, Shawn, and their two preschoolers.

"Number One Fan," by Donna Linville as told to B.J. Connor. Used by permission. All rights reserved. B.J. Connor thanks God for her inspiring, encouraging mother, Virginia Worth Nichol. B.J. (Betty Jo) has won an Amy Writing Award and has been published in books, magazines, and newspapers. She and her husband, Michael, have two children, Nichole and Sean, and have provided foster care for four newborns. They make their home in Ann Arbor, Michigan.

"Tucked In," by Rachel Wallace-Oberle. Copyright © 2002. Used by permission. All rights reserved. Rachel Wallace-Oberle has an education in Radio/Television Broadcasting as well as Journalism/Print. She is a freelance writer and has written for numerous publications. One of her favorite topics to write about is her family. Rachel also co-hosts a weekly Christian radio program. In her spare time she loves walking, classical music, and canaries.

"Be At the Gate," by Ellie Lofaro. Copyright © 2001. Used by permission. All rights reserved. Ellie Lofaro has touched the hearts and funny bones of audiences since 1984. Her accomplishments include ten years teaching high school English and two years as the host of a daily live talk show in New York. *Slices of Life* is her first book (Cook Communications, 2002). She has also written for *Today's Christian Woman*, Zondervan, and Word.

The Comfort of a Mother

"Someone to Come Home To" excerpts taken from *First We Have Coffee*, by Margaret Jensen. Copyright © 1995 by Harvest House Publishers, Eugene, OR 97402. Used by permission. All rights reserved.

"Adventuring with God," taken from *Beside a Quiet Stream: Words of Hope for Weary Hearts*, by Penelope J. Stokes. Copyright © 1999 by Penelope J. Stokes. Used by permission of J. Countryman, a division of Thomas Nelson, Inc. All rights reserved.

"As a Little Child," excerpted from *The Eyes of the Heart* by Tracie Peterson. Copyright © 2002 by Tracie Peterson. Used by permission of Bethany House Publishers. All rights reserved.

"Mother As Comforter," excerpted from *Mothers & Daughters* by Marie Chapian. Copyright © 1988 by Marie Chapian. Used by permission of Bethany House Publishers. All rights reserved.

"The Great Coverer," by Candy Arrington. Copyright © 2002. Used by permission. All rights reserved. Candy Arrington is a freelance author, whose publishing credits include *Angels On Earth, War Cry, Discipleship Journal, Christian Home & School, The Upper Room,* and *Focus On the Family.* She is coauthoring *Aftershock: Help, Hope, and Healing Following Suicide,* scheduled for release in 2003. Candy lives in Spartanburg, South Carolina.

"The Distant Rumble," taken from *Honestly* by Sheila Walsh. Copyright © 1996 by Sheila Walsh. Used by permission of Zondervan. All rights reserved.

The Strength of a Mother

"Fork in the Road," by Phil Callaway. Excerpt taken from *I Used to Have Answers, Now I Have Kids.* Copyright © 2000 by Phil Callaway. Published by Harvest House Publishers, Eugene, OR 97402. Used by permission. All rights reserved.

"A Mother's Discipline," by Birdie Etchison. Copyright © 2002. Used by permission. All rights reserved. Birdie Etchison writes inspirational romance and nonfiction for a variety of publishers. She enjoys travel, conducting writer's seminars, and has been co-director of Writer's Weekend at the Beach for the past twelve years. She resides on the beautiful Washington coast.

"What Mothers Are For," by Aletheia Lee Butler. Copyright © 2002. Used by permission. All rights reserved. Aletheia Lee Butler is a fourth grade teacher in Douglasville, Georgia. She has had three poems published by the National Library of Poetry. She thanks God every day for the gift of her loving parents. Her story is dedicated to the memory of her mother, Catherine Sennett Lee. Aletheia lives in East Point with her husband, Jason.

"Tommy's Triumph," by Kathy Ide. Copyright © 2002. Used by permission. All rights reserved. Kathy Ide does freelance proofreading, editing, critiquing, and coauthoring for individuals, editing networks, and Christian book publishers. She has been a published author of magazine articles, playscripts, short stories, devotionals, and Sunday school curricula since 1988.

"Visibility," taken from *Fearfully and Wonderfully Made,* by Philip D. Yancey and Paul W. Brand. Copyright © 1980 by Paul Brand and Philip Yancey. Used by permission of Zondervan. All rights reserved.

The Presence of a Mother

The Unconditional Love of a Mother

children for eleven years and also taught drama and creative writing at a school of the arts for Christian homeschoolers. Janice is the director of a drama ministry team called "Out There!" Ministries, which travels the globe spreading the gospel message through drama. Janice and her husband reside in the Houston area. They have four daughters.

ENCOURAGE *the* SOUL,
ENLIGHTEN *the* MIND,
EMBOLDEN *the* HEART

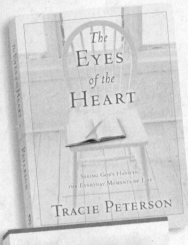

Grasp God's Presence in Everyday Life

Using moments from her own life, Tracie Peterson reassures you that God can and will be found in the details of life. From this simple discovery she'll help lead you to a more vital, overflowing relationship with Him.

The Eyes of the Heart
by Tracie Peterson

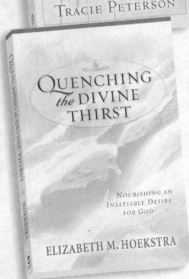

Nourishing Our Desire for God

"Living water." Jesus promised it to the woman at the well, and it is a promise made for all of us. Using this encounter, His walk on water, the wedding at Cana, the invalid at the pool of Bethesda, and other biblical illustrations, Elizabeth Hoekstra offers fresh insight into how we can experience the blessings and promises God pours out.

Quenching the Divine Thirst
by Elizabeth M. Hoekstra

◆ BETHANYHOUSE